Fantastic Vocation!

Fantastic Vocation!

Father Joseph A. Miksch

To order additional copies of this book, contact:
Xlibris Corporation
1-888-795-4274
www.Xlibris.com
Orders@Xlibris.com
71378

CONTENTS

FOREWORD

FATHER MIKSCH HAS found one of the secrets of spiritual life. God can be found in the ordinary events of life. It's delightful to read how he sees God in the typical experiences of the day-to-day life of a priest. What is so ordinary is still the place for experiencing the joy of God's presence. What may appear to be ho-hum stories of people at the rectory door, or people in hurting situations, is really the revelation of God's presence. Read a few of his stories and then reflect upon how God can be present in the same way in your life.

Some think they must go to the mountaintops or the far away deserts to experience God. Father Miksch reminds us that God is at the front door, the parking lot, in the emergency hospital call in the middle of the night, and in the stories of people.

Father Joe has demonstrated that priests do find God in ordinary ways and thus they are happy and spiritual people. For him, life is not a grim grinding out of daily schedules but a life of serenity. It's good news for priests and it's good news for lay people. The spirituality of God in the ordinary stories of life is a good lesson for all, priests and laity.

Most Reverend William J. Dendinger
Bishop of Grand Island

INTRODUCTION

H AVE YOU EVER wondered what other people do all day? You work hard for long hours each day, but what do others do? Ever wish you could trade places with others? So many people have such easy jobs!

The grass always seems to be greener on the other side of the fence. Have you ever looked at others and thought, "Gee! They really have it made! How I wish I could be in their shoes!"

Wouldn't it be great if one could just get away from the pressure of one's duties and be a cross-country truck driver! How nice it would be to pull an 18-wheeler out onto the interstate and drive to California. No worries! No hassle! Beautiful scenery along the way!

Any long-haul truck driver would tell you it's not so, especially today with the high cost of fuel. Still, there are days when it's nice to fantasize and think how wonderful it would be to be a truck driver!

Over the years I've heard people say, "Teachers really have it made! They are off throughout the summer months, get a nice break at Christmas, work from 8:00 a.m. to 4:00 p.m. What a cushy job!"

Don't ever say that to a teacher! Yes! They may get summers off, but most likely they are attending summer school to keep up their certification. They are in the school building from 8:00 a.m. till 4:00 p.m., but spend most evenings and weekends planning lessons for the next day and correcting papers, and are involved with numerous other extracurricular activities.

Over the years I've had a number of different kinds of jobs, some for only a short time, but long enough to get a taste of what it would be like to work full time at such jobs. I grew up on a farm, so know something about agriculture. As a teenager, I used to love spending long hours in the field, plowing or cultivating corn. I discovered, however, that it isn't so much fun when machinery breaks down, the weather is bad, or farm prices are low.

I worked on an assembly line for the railroad one summer building boxcars. My job was bucking rivets. Doing the same thing all day, day after day, I have never been more bored in all my life!

As a private pilot, I've flown enough to realize that after the initial excitement of flying wears off, flying an airplane can become rather routine and boring. Sure, there are moments of excitement, flying through storms, for example, but there are also many hours of boredom. While I do enjoy going on long cross-country flights from time to time, I think I would find it rather boring if I were a pilot and had to fly every day.

I spent four summers working for the Department of the Interior in one of our national parks. For a young man this was a wonderful way to spend one's summer. Hiking beautiful mountain trails, clearing downed timber, shoveling snow, and encountering bears and other forms of wildlife were truly an adventure. But as I reflect back on those days, I also remember working out in the rain on muddy trails, wet and cold, and sleeping on hard cots in tents in the backcountry. Sure, there was excitement, but there were many times when we were downright miserable.

The grass may appear to be greener on the other side of the fence, but my limited experience has taught me that no matter how glamorous a job may seem to be from the outside, there are always pressures and unpleasantness which go with it. When one is tempted to think that other people have it made, it's good to pause and take a second look.

So what's my job?

I'm a Catholic priest. I've spent the past forty-three years of my life as a parish priest. Without a doubt I have the greatest job in the whole world, and I wouldn't trade it for any other!

So what do priests do all day?

Many people seem to think that all a priest does is say Mass each morning and on weekends, pray, and take naps. Yes! Take naps! I wonder how many times over the years when I didn't answer the doorbell or pick up the telephone immediately, I was greeted with "Oh, Father, did I wake you from your nap?"

Just what do priests do all day? Why would anyone want to become a priest? Doesn't sitting around the rectory and praying all day become rather boring?

Not for this priest! I've had my share of excitement and adventure in life! As a pilot, I've made several emergency landings. As a rock climber, I've had incredible thrills climbing mountains in the United States and abroad. Working in the backcountry, I've tangled with bears and once charged a moose. Exciting? You better believe it! But none of these experiences compare

FATHER JOSEPH A. MIKSCH

to the excitement and thrills I have experienced as a priest. For me, my forty-three years as a Catholic priest have been one fantastic, adventuresome, and exciting journey!

In this book filled with anecdotes, I hope to share some of the daily adventures in the life of a priest, thus giving you a better understanding as to just what a priest does do all day.

A TYPICAL DAY

I F THERE IS one thing I have learned as a priest, it has been that of learning how to deal with interruptions. The telephone and the doorbell ring at all hours of the day or night. It may be an emergency, a wrong number, or an unannounced visit from a friend one hasn't seen for years.

Sometimes when people call, especially late at night, one has to wonder if they are thinking at all. When my phone rings at 2:00 a.m., I think of emergencies—an accident or someone dying in the hospital. I jump out of bed, stumble over a chair, stub my toe, and breathlessly pick up the receiver to hear someone ask: "Oh, Father! Did I wake you?"

"Of course you woke me! What do most normal people do at 2:00 a.m.?" I don't say that, but I certainly think it!

"Father, I was just calling to see what time your Masses are on Sunday." (The Mass times are printed in the yellow pages of the telephone directory right next to the phone number, but no one ever seems to notice.)

In one parish where I was stationed for a number of years, the parish phone number was xx4-xxxx, and the local bar's number was xx3-xxxx. Three or four nights a week I would get calls at the rectory between midnight and 1:00 a.m. I would pick up the receiver, thinking it was an emergency, only to be asked if so-and-so was still there.

At first, after receiving such calls, I would return to bed, but I would be so upset over the interruption of my sleep that I would lie awake and simmer for several hours, but gradually I learned to be grateful that it was not an emergency and that I didn't have to go out. With such an attitude I could fall back to sleep within minutes.

Then, one night, the thought occurred to me: What about my reputation? Every time someone calls the bar late at night, Father Joe answers! Thinking such thoughts, I could laugh when my sleep was interrupted by such calls.

I have a cousin with the same name as I. Sometimes people dial his number late at night to see if I would bail them out of jail. I often wonder what they think when his wife answers!

Sometimes on a "typical day," it takes me all morning to type a simple one-page letter because there are so many interruptions.

So what kind of interruptions might they be? It might be a distraught person who has recently gone through a bitter divorce and needs to talk. It might be someone who has just been diagnosed with a serious illness, or whose loved one has just been killed in a car accident. It might be a parent distraught over a child's abuse of drugs or alcohol. It might be a person who needs to rent money to avoid being evicted from an apartment. The list could go on and on. One never knows where a telephone call or doorbell might lead; such interruptions might be the beginning of a new relationship that will last for the rest of one's life. This is what is so exciting about being a priest!

So what's a typical day like in the life of a priest? If there is such a day, it might be something like this: I usually climb out of bed at 6:00 a.m. With a cup of coffee nearby, I spend perhaps a half hour in prayer and reflection. I've learned over the years that if I don't take this quiet time early in the morning to pray, I may never have time to pray.

Breakfast follows with the morning news on TV; then some time is spent in preparation for the celebration of Mass at 8:10 a.m. After Mass I usually spend an hour in school, teaching religion to our grade school students.

But even in the classroom one is not spared from interruptions! Once I was called from the room by the principal for an emergency phone call. A young man, strung out on drugs in his basement home, was threatening to kill himself or anyone who attempted to come down and talk to him. His mother wanted to know if I would please come and talk to him.

For some unknown reason I really didn't want to leave the classrooms that day. I was really enjoying teaching!

Walking slowly down the steps, assuring him that I meant no harm, a thought occurred to me: If he does shoot me, that really wouldn't be too bad—"Saint Father Joe, priest and martyr!" After all, I would be giving my life in the line of duty.

On other occasions I have been called from the classroom to rush to the scene of a fatal accident, the nursing home, or hospital where someone was dying. One priest I know climbed the town water tower to talk a person out of jumping.

On a "typical day," after teaching for an hour or so, I will check my mail and spend perhaps an hour taking care of office business, answering phone calls and messages left by the secretary. Frequently someone is waiting to see me. An appointment or two before lunch and already the day is half over.

FATHER JOSEPH A. MIKSCH

I tend to become sleepy after lunch, so that's when I venture out to visit the sick in hospitals, nursing home, and in their own homes. This is perhaps the most rewarding part of my day. The sick and homebound are so grateful and appreciative for such visits and treasure the opportunity to receive our Lord in the Eucharist.

Many priests are avid golfers, so they spend part of the afternoon on the golf course. I played my last round of golf in 1957 and concluded that my game was about as good as it was ever going to be, so I gave up the sport. Instead I vent my frustrations chopping out tree stumps with an ax, wedges, and a sledgehammer. One winter I spent many hours in an elderly woman's backyard chopping out twenty stumps. A Lutheran pastor in town had a fireplace, so he raked up the chips and burned them. Not many people can boast about having a priest and a minister cleaning up their backyard!

Late afternoons are filled with appointments; evenings are always booked with programs such as RCIA (instructions for adults interested in joining the church), parish religious education programs for children, adult education programs, marriage prep sessions with engaged couples, and countless meetings. Usually my day doesn't begin to slow down until around 9:30 p.m.

After some time in prayer, I like to watch the late news, then relax and unwind for another half hour before retiring around 11:00 p.m. Such is a typical day in my life.

There are some days during the summer months when things aren't quite so hectic. Occasionally there is a day in which little happens, and for a short while I can find life to be "boring," but such days are few and far between.

National holidays are the greatest! Although thoughtful and considerate parishioners invite me to their homes on such days to celebrate with them, I prefer to remain at home in the rectory and enjoy the peace and quiet. Only on such days is the telephone silent and the doorbell doesn't ring!

Then there are times when everything seems to happen. I remember once such occasion: After teaching all morning in our high school, I drove to the hospital in a neighboring town to attend a seminar on ministering to the terminally ill and their families. The seminar was over at 5:30 p.m. Before grabbing a bite to eat, I visited parishioners who were in the hospital, and then attended an ecumenical meeting of local clergymen. This meeting was over at 9:30 p.m. Arriving back home at 10:30 p.m., I was tired and worn out. It had been a long and exhausting day!

I planned to say the evening prayer and then relax for a few minutes before going to bed. The phone rang before I finished my evening prayer.

An elderly woman exclaimed frantically: "Oh, thank God, you are finally back, Father! I've been trying to get a hold of you all evening." She went on to explain that her husband, who had been in the hospital for several days, had taken a turn for the worse. She didn't feel comfortable driving one hundred miles to the "big city" alone and wanted to know if I knew someone who could take her down to see him. Rather than bother someone else so late at night, I offered to take her down myself.

We arrived at the hospital at 1:00 a.m. I stayed with her and her husband until 4:00 a.m., at which time I told them that I had to head back for morning Mass. She decided to stay with her husband. When she was ready to return home, I assured her that I would find a ride for her.

Arriving back at the rectory at 6:00 a.m., I set several alarm clocks for 7:30 a.m. and flopped down on my bed, hoping to get an hour's sleep before Mass. Minutes later the phone rang. A young man had been involved in a car accident on his way to work and was in critical condition; could I come to the hospital! Splashing some cold water on my face in an effort to wake up, I rushed to the hospital and anointed the young man. Spending some time with his parents in the waiting room, I then rushed back to celebrate the morning Mass.

Calling the hospital after Mass to check on the young man's condition, I learned that he had died, so I spent the rest of the morning with his parents and family. When I returned to the rectory at noon, having been awake for thirty hours, I sat down in an easy chair and fell asleep. Half an hour later the doorbell rang. It took awhile for me to run down the stairs and a long hallway. When I opened the door, a woman greeted me with: "Oh, Father, did I wake you from your nap?"

I recall another time after a busy week I was looking forward to Sunday afternoon and a somewhat relaxing and easy week thereafter. A dear friend celebrated her nineteenth birthday that Sunday afternoon. Driving home from the enjoyable celebration, I was looking forward to a relaxing evening and a week ahead with few appointments.

Arriving back at the rectory, I noticed the red light was blinking on the answering machine. Checking the message, I was horrified to hear that three young men, two of whom were from my parish, had been killed in an auto accident. I went first to spend some time with one family, accompanying the father of one of the boys to the local mortuary where he identified the body of his son. I'll never forget that experience! What can one say on such an occasion! I know I can't begin to imagine what goes through a parent's mind on such an occasion! I know this dad would gladly and without hesitation have given his own life if he could have brought his son back.

Nor will I ever forget going to the mortuary several days later and seeing the boy's mother kneeling before his casket. Seeing her pain gave me an insight to the suffering and pain Mary must have felt as she stood at the foot of the cross. Only she could understand what was going through this poor mother's mind!

We buried one of the boys on Tuesday and the other on Wednesday. In the meanwhile, a good friend of mine, from a nearby parish where I had once served as pastor, also died. A double amputee who has suffered much in recent years, his death was a comforting experience for his family, knowing that his life of suffering was finally over. Since their pastor was away on retreat, the family asked if I would officiate at his funeral liturgy on Thursday, which I felt honored to do. Wednesday evening we celebrated the vigil, and then went to the parish hall for coffee and to socialize with the family. While there, the phone rang. It was a call from the local mortuary. A young man from my parish had just taken his life.

Rushing to the mortuary, I said the prayers for the dead over him, and then went to console his parents, brother, and sister. Tragic as was the accidental deaths of the three young men earlier in the week, this death was an even greater tragedy!

The vigil service for this young man was on Friday evening, and his funeral was on Saturday morning. I also had a wedding scheduled for that Saturday afternoon. Thus, Friday evening I went from the joyful and jovial wedding rehearsal to the sad and somber vigil. Next morning I officiated at the funeral liturgy and committal service in the cemetery and then went on to the joyful wedding celebration. It is difficult to shift back and forth from such emotional extremes.

After the wedding Mass, I heard confessions for several hours and then celebrated the weekend liturgy. By this time I was mentally and emotionally exhausted. My sister and her family, who seldom have an opportunity to attend one of the liturgies at which I officiate, were present, but I didn't even notice them in the congregation. Nor did we visit afterward; they realized I was too emotionally and physically drained.

Fortunately, there are not many weeks as hectic as this, but they do occur from time to time. Recently I decided to keep a record of my appointments and activities during a more typical week. What follows is a summary of that "typical week."

Sunday:

Up at	6:00 a.m.	Dress, unlock church, pray
	7:00 a.m.	Mass
	8:00 a.m.	Breakfast
	9:00 a.m.	Mass
	11:00 a.m.	Mass
Noon—	3:00 p.m.	Second marriage class
	4:00 p.m.	Communion service with my sister
	7:00 p.m.	Stained glass window committee meeting
	8:00 p.m.	First chance to relax!
	8:30 p.m.	Phone call: Hospital emergency
	10:00 p.m.	Back from hospital, relax till bed time.

Monday:

Up at	6:00 a.m.	Dress, unlock church, breakfast, pray
	8:10 a.m.	Mass
	9:00 a.m.	Appointment with eye doctor
	10:30 a.m.	Hospital visitation
	11:30 a.m.	Visit with college student discerning vocation and lunch with him
	1:00 p.m.	Visit to jail
	2:00 p.m.	Marriage prep
	3:00 p.m.	Appointment with a young man seeking help and advice to remodel and make livable his home
	4:30 p.m.	Appointment with a person whose marriage is going on the rocks
	5:30 p.m.	Meeting with school board
	6:20 p.m.	Chance to have a sandwich
	7:00 p.m.	RCIA classes
	9:00 p.m.	Work with person on annulment procedures
	10:00 p.m.	Counseling session on telephone
	10:30 p.m.	After a full day, time for bed

FATHER JOSEPH A. MIKSCH

Tuesday:

Up at	6:00 a.m.	Dress, unlock church, breakfast, pray
	8:10 a.m.	Mass
	9:00 a.m.	Visit first-grade classroom
	9:30 a.m.	Visit fourth-grade classroom
	9:50 a.m.	Called from classroom to hospital where someone is dying
	10:30 a.m.	Counseling session with someone who was stressed out with a new job
	Noon:	Luncheon and school endowment board meeting
	1:00 p.m.	Visit prisoner in jail with letter for him to present to the judge
	2:00 p.m.	Meeting with a couple about annulment
	3:00 p.m.	Visit elderly in the nursing home
	4:00 p.m.	Office work and phone calls
	4:30 p.m.	Meeting on dealing with pornography
	4:45 p.m.	Time for prayer
	5:00 p.m.	Dinner
	6:00 p.m.	Finance council meeting
	7:00 p.m.	Pastoral council meeting
	8:15 p.m.	Ultreya meeting
	9:45 p.m.	Chance to relax
	10:30 p.m.	Time for bed

Wednesday:

Up at	6:00 a.m.	Dress, unlock church, breakfast, pray
	8:10 a.m.	Mass
	9:00-11:00 a.m.	Habitat for Humanity site
	11:00 a.m.	Visit kindergarten classroom
	11:30 p.m.	Visit third-grade classroom
	12:00 p.m.	Bite to eat with faculty
	12:30 p.m.	Lunch with children to discuss their mother's readiness to enter a nursing home

	2:00 p.m.	Visit second-grade classroom
	2:45 p.m.	Anointing at nursing home
	4:00 p.m.	Marriage prep
	5:00 p.m.	Visit with a family to plan funeral liturgy
	6:00 p.m.	Serving practice with PRE kids
	6:30-8:00 p.m.	PRE
	8:15 p.m.	Marriage prep
	9:45 p.m.	Chance to relax and eat supper
	10:20 p.m.	Phone call counseling, loan $200
	10:30 p.m.	Chance to relax, pray, and retire

Thursday:

Up at	6:00 a.m.	Dress, unlock church, breakfast, pray
	8:10 a.m.	Mass
	9:25 a.m.	Left for funeral at Morris Bluff
	12:45 p.m.	Home visit of an elderly man whose toes had recently been amputated
	1:15 p.m.	Lunch
	1:30 p.m.	Answered a pile of phone calls and wrote two letters of recommendation for seniors applying for scholarships
	2:15 p.m.	Couple dropped by to seek advice on dealing with nephew in the pen
	2:45 p.m.	Phone call for advice about bailing someone out of county jail for DUI
	3:00 p.m.	Met with a family at mortuary
	4:05 p.m.	First chance to relax for a few minutes
	4:20 p.m.	Wrote a letter to a fellow in the Lincoln pen
	4:30 p.m.	Confirmation interview
	5:20 p.m.	Dinner
	6:30 p.m.	Church to prepare for vigil service
	7:00 p.m.	Vigil Service
	8:00 p.m.	Counseling session
	9:00 p.m.	Day is finally finished, relaxed, looked at funeral liturgy readings
	10:00 p.m.	Phone call
	10:30 p.m.	To bed

Friday:

Up at	6:00 a.m.	Dress, unlock church, breakfast, prayer, work on funeral homily
	8:10 a.m.	Mass
	9:00 a.m.	Work on funeral homily
	10:30 a.m.	Funeral liturgy
	12:00 p.m.	Funeral dinner
	1:00 p.m.	Focus—Marriage prep
	2:30 p.m.	Home Mass with my sister
	4:00 p.m.	Office work and weekend liturgy prep
	6:00 p.m.	Wedding rehearsal
	7:00 p.m.	Prenuptial dinner
	8:10 a.m.	Leave for Tintern for grace talk
	1:00 a.m.	To bed

Saturday:

Up at	6:00 a.m.	Dress, unlock church, breakfast, prayer
	8:10 a.m.	Morning Mass
	9:00 a.m.	Appointment
	10:00 a.m.	Church to prepare for wedding
	11:00 a.m.	Wedding
	1:00-3:00 p.m.	Free—Prepare weekend homily
	3:30-5:00 p.m.	Confessions
	5:30 p.m.	Mass
	6:30 p.m.	Marriage validation
	7:00 p.m.	Dinner at the Elks Country Club
	8:30 p.m.	Finally, a chance to relax

Sunday:

Up at	5:30 a.m.	Dress, unlock church, prayer
	7:00 a.m.	Mass
	8:00 a.m.	Breakfast
	9:00 a.m.	Prayer
	10:00 a.m.	Work on Pauline Privilege case
	11:00 a.m.	Mass

12:00 p.m.	Baptism
1:00 p.m.	Family ministry marriage program
2:00 p.m.	First reconciliation
4:00 p.m.	Marriage validation
5:00 p.m.	Soup supper
5:30 p.m.	Head to Norfolk for CEC closing
10:15 p.m.	Back home
11:00 p.m.	To bed

I was once visiting with a parishioner who expressed the hope that her son might choose to become a priest. During the course of our conversation, she said to me, "It must be nice to have a job in which you can touch people's lives and really make a difference!"

I am so grateful for that statement; it really helps me put my priesthood in perspective. I truly do have a job in which I can touch people's lives and really make a difference. After such grueling days as the ones just described above, and at the end of a "typical" day, I can look back with a deep sense of satisfaction, knowing that I have touched some people's lives and have truly made a difference.

Sometimes the visitor at the door also touches my life and really makes a difference—a small child, for example, with a bouquet of dandelions for Father, the memory of which may bring smiles for years to come!

By the way, did I ever tell you that dandelions are my favorite flower?

FATHER JOSEPH A. MIKSCH

CHRISTIANS SHOULD BE MORE LIKE DANDELIONS

E VEN AS A little child I was taught to hate those ugly little yellow flowers which poked their heads up everywhere in our beautiful green lawn, flower garden, and yard. We dug them out, pulled them out, mowed them down, and sprayed them with toxic poisons. Just when we thought we had seen the last of them, they would reappear, unintimidated, proudly displaying their brilliant yellow flowers.

The war to exterminate dandelions still continues. I see people everywhere spraying, mowing, and chopping out these

Dreaded weeds with little success. It seems that for each one killed, a hundred grow up in its place. In spite of our efforts to eliminate them from our lawns, most of us eventually come to realize that we will have to learn to coexist. Dandelions are here to stay!

In recent years I've come to realize that my attitude toward dandelions is gradually changing. Once I looked upon them as an ugly and dreaded weed to be destroyed, whereas today I find that I am beginning to admire them. Upon closer examination they really are a beautiful, bright yellow flower. And I admire their courage! With everyone trying to exterminate them, one would think they would try to camouflage themselves so that they would blend in with the grass. If their flowers were green, for example, we would scarcely notice them and then we could coexist peacefully. But no! They choose to remain a bright yellow so that they stand out in our lawns and can be seen from a great distance.

In spite of the fact that no one likes them, dandelions also have some useful purposes. Their leaves are eatable as a green salad, their flowers make a delicious and potent wine, and what child hasn't enjoyed smearing their "butter" on the cheek or chin of a friend or made a chain-link necklace out of their long stems. Still the battle to stamp out dandelions continues!

As I was watching a man walking through his lawn with a sprayer, meticulously dousing each bright yellow flowering plant, the thought occurred to me: Wouldn't it be great if we who profess to be Christians had the courage to profess and proclaim our faith to those around us in the same way in which dandelions share their bright flowers with us?

Some years ago I read a brief thought-provoking statement: *If you were accused of being a Christian, would there be enough evidence to convict you?* Sometimes we work with people for months before discovering that they are Catholic; sometimes others work with us for months too before discovering that we are Catholic. Not a word is said about our faith or beliefs, in fact, we avoid such topics like the plague.

I recall being self-conscious and shy about praying before meals in public back in the days when I was in college. Then one day I got to thinking about the hippies who were just beginning to proclaim their anticultural values in dress, habits, and speech. If they had the courage to proclaim such antiestablishment and strange beliefs, why should I be ashamed to let people know that I am a believer in Jesus Christ! I no longer hesitate to make the sign of the cross in public when I pray before meals, and I admire others when I see them doing the same.

A Catholic friend of mine who attended a Lutheran college was telling me about her experiences while attending weekly prayer services at the college chapel. At first when prayers began with the words: "In the name of the Father, and of the Son, and of the Holy Spirit," she was reluctant to make the sign of the cross. Then one day she thought: "Protestants aren't ashamed to proclaim their differences in beliefs when they attend Catholic services; they remain seated when everyone else stands or kneels." From that time onward she began making the sign of the cross. Within a week she noticed that seven other students, who had been attending services regularly, were doing likewise. Several even came up to her and said, "I didn't know you were Catholic."

On another occasion while taking a scripture course the discussion centered around the wedding at Cana in John's Gospel. As they read through the narrative, it suddenly dawned on her, a convert to Catholicism from Lutheranism, that even before Jesus's time had come, Mary was already acting as an intercessor on behalf of the wedding couple. Mary informed Jesus of the crisis: "They have no more wine." Then she told the servants: "Do whatever He tells you!"

Overwhelmed with excitement by this insight, she shared it with her professor before the entire class. A hushed silence fell upon everyone. The professor, a kind and gentle man, merely smiled and said, "But we don't believe in Mary as an intercessor!"

Feeling the eyes of everyone fixed upon her, my friend looked at the professor and replied, "But I do!"

It took more than a bit of courage to make the sign of the cross at prayer services and to stand up for her convictions in the classroom, but before long a number of students were coming up to her to ask questions about Catholic beliefs or to explain what the rosary was all about. And often, after sharing of her beliefs, they would exclaim, "Gee, that's really cool! No one ever explained it to me that way before!"

At the end of the semester while visiting with her scripture professor, he commented: "Are you aware of the fact that by your presence on our campus, you have caused a lot of consternation in our theology department! Our professors were unable to keep on schedule and cover all the material they had hoped to because of all the questions students were raising after conversing with you. But it has been a wonderful experience for all of us. We can only grow in our faith when we are willing to take the risk of defending it. I don't agree with all of your beliefs, but I truly respect you for the way you have grown in your faith, and I truly appreciate the way you have challenged us to grow in ours!"

When my friend graduated, she was awarded the student of the year award, truly a prestigious award for a Catholic student to receive from a Lutheran college.

In the early days of Christianity and down through the centuries many Christians have had the courage to profess their faith in spite of persecution. In fact, the Roman emperors discovered that Christians were very much like dandelions. For everyone they crucified, fed to lions, or burned at the stake, ten more stepped forward to take their places. In our own times we again are witnessing the triumph of Catholicism and Christianity over anti-Christian dictatorial regimes. Dubbed as the "opium of the people," Christianity was oppressed for many years under Communistic socialism. Today we see the collapse of Communistic forms of government, but the faith is still strong and ready to blossom once again. Christians, like dandelions, are difficult to eradicate!

Now when I see dandelions displaying their yellow flowers brilliantly in my lawn, I no longer think of them as nasty weeds, but I'm reminded that I need to proclaim my faith boldly to those around me even if others don't necessarily care to hear about the message and values of Jesus. Perhaps we should even adopt the dandelion as a Christian symbol!

FATHER JOSEPH A. MIKSCH

A PRIEST'S GREATEST JOY

IT HAD BEEN another long and tiring day; I was mentally and emotionally exhausted. I retired at 11:00 p.m. and fell asleep within minutes. At eleven thirty the phone began to ring. It rang several times before I realized what was happening. Fumbling around in the dark to find the light switch, I managed to get to the phone on the fifth ring.

"Father, I'm sorry to be bothering you at this late hour, but I really need to talk to you. Can I please come over?"

Normally I would have asked a person calling so late to come for an appointment in the morning, but it was obvious from the distress in his voice that he needed to talk to me immediately. I replied, "Sure! Come right over if you feel it's an emergency."

Fully awake by this time, I dressed and went to my office to wait for the caller. He arrived a few minutes later and apologized again for coming in the middle of the night. He was extremely nervous; there was a tremor in his voice. He couldn't look me in the eye but kept looking down at the floor or up at the ceiling. For the longest time I had no idea why he had come. Our conversation seemed to be leading nowhere, but eventually he managed to blurt out the fact that he wanted to go to confession.

Painfully, he began to reveal his life story. At times it seemed as though he simply would not be able to go on. For some twenty-four years he had stayed away from church convinced that he would never have the strength and the courage to tell his story to anyone. With each long pause, I found myself praying to God to give him the grace to continue. Tears of compassion welled up in my eyes as I tried to reassure him that it was okay; I wouldn't condemn him no matter what he told me.

Finally there was no more to tell. What he had struggled with for so many years, what he could hardly admit even to himself, and what he felt he would never be able to tell to another human being, finally had all been spilled out. Tears flowed freely now as he sobbed uncontrollably.

Gradually he regained his composure as I began to share with him the Gospel stories of Jesus dealing with sinners: the story of the prodigal son, the woman taken in adultery, and the prayer of forgiveness which Jesus prayed from the cross. This same Jesus was willing and eager to forgive his sins too. We prayed together for a few minutes and then I said the prayer of absolution, the prayer he had longed to hear for so many years.

We continued to converse for quite some time. He told me that he hadn't slept for the past two days, and that he had been unable to concentrate on his work or keep his mind on anything. He had gone to bed that night, but came to realize that sleep would be impossible. Finally, he made up his mind to call me right then and there to see if he could come and talk things over. He went on to tell me that for the past twenty-four years he had always gone to bed at night worrying about his relationship with God and praying that someday he would have the courage to confess his sins and make his peace with God, but never thinking that he would ever be able to do so.

Now he sat there with tears in his eyes, so very much relieved, happy, and at peace. I too had tears in my eyes as I listened to him and reassured him that his horrible nightmare was now over, that God had forgiven him long ago and that he could go in peace.

When he got up to leave sometime after 2:00 a.m., I reached out to shake his hand, but found myself embracing him instead. We both shed tears of pure joy, and then said "Good night!"

I didn't go back to bed until after 4:00 a.m. I knew it would be futile to try to go to sleep. My heart was pounding for joy as I paced back and forth in my room, thanking God for the privilege I had just had in bringing His peace to a troubled soul. I wanted to shout out and proclaim to the whole world what a glorious event had just taken place.

And all the while I kept thinking back on the transformation which had taken place in this man's life during the course of two and a half hours. The nervous, distraught, and troubled person who walked into my office practically floated out of the room when he left; he was so happy, so relieved, so filled with joy and peace for the first time in twenty-four years.

Several weeks later a beautiful thing happened. It was Easter Sunday and crowds of people jammed into our church for Mass. Twenty minutes before Mass was scheduled to begin, people were already standing outside the doorways unable to get in.

After Mass, as I stood just outside the main doors of the church and greeted people as they passed by, I caught sight of the man who had come to me in the middle of the night. He had slipped out one of the side doors and was making his way against the flow of traffic toward me. When he got up to me, he merely shook my hand, looked me right in the eye, and said, "Happy Easter, Father!" Then he walked away.

Tears still come to my eyes as I recall that moment. No Easter greeting has ever meant more to me! He truly had found his peace with God. Jesus had truly risen and was alive in his heart. I shall never forget that experience!

As I reflect back upon this experience, several thoughts come to mind. First of all, I feel very close to this man even though I do not know his name. I can honestly say that I love him. Whenever people trust me enough to share the secrets of their lives, I can only respond with love.

It amazes me, too, to realize that I seldom remember the sins people confess to me. Perhaps this is because there is nothing unusual about most people's sins, including my own—it's really difficult to commit an "original" sin.

What I do remember is the transformation which takes place during the course of our conversation—a very troubled and distraught person comes to me, and a radiant and joyful person leaves. Sometimes in the course of a few minutes I witness a change that a psychiatrist or psychologist works for years to see. What an extraordinary privilege I have as a priest to be a minister of the sacrament of penance and reconciliation and to witness such a transformation in another person.

Because of the many similar experiences I've had as a priest, I've come to realize what a tremendous gift we Catholics have in the sacrament of penance. I'm absolutely convinced that Jesus knew our psychological needs much better than we ourselves do when He gave the church this sacrament.

In my own mind I am convinced that God had forgiven the man mentioned above long before he came to talk to me, but he needed to share his guilt, his sins, with me in order to find peace. He needed to be reassured by me, another human being, that God had forgiven him, that he could leave the past behind and make a new beginning. Many psychologists have written of this need we have to share our sins and our guilt with another person before we can leave them behind.

On some occasions, too, a priest may be able to offer some advice, which may help one to grow in the practice of Christian virtue. I remember one such bit of advice that I once was given while receiving the sacrament of penance. I had confessed being impatient with people on the telephone. Calls at an inopportune moment would sometimes trigger an impatient response or tone of voice.

Fortunately, my confessor didn't tell me just to pray the usual "three Hail Marys" for my penance. Instead he asked me if I would do the following: "Before picking up the receiver, just pause for a moment and consider that perhaps someone is calling who has never called a priest before. Perhaps he wants to inquire about joining the church. Or maybe a person who has been away from the church for many years has finally mustered up enough courage to call a priest to see if he could come over to receive the sacrament of penance. If you indicate by the tone of your voice that you are impatient or angry, that person may hang up and never bother to call a priest again. So just think about that throughout this coming week before you pick up the receiver."

I made that confession forty years ago, but it still works. Whenever the phone rings at an inopportune moment, I recall those words and calm down before picking up the receiver. Because of this confession I am a better person and a more effective priest today.

I suppose the greatest reason why so many people are apprehensive about receiving the sacrament of penance is that they feel ashamed and embarrassed when confessing their sins to a priest. What will Father think of me?

From the incident I have already described, it ought to be apparent what I think and how I feel when someone comes and unloads a heavy burden of sin. I can sense almost immediately how difficult it is for that person to come to me. The quivering voice, the nervous tension, the tears—all betray the anguish in the heart.

In some cases I know that it has taken many months, even years, for a person to muster up enough courage to come to confession. In such cases my instant reaction is one of much compassion, empathy, patience, and understanding. After all, I too am a sinner and have been in similar situations. As the author of the letter to the Hebrews says: "He [the priest] is able to deal patiently with erring sinners, for he himself is beset by weakness" (5:2).

Realizing, too, how much mental anguish the penitent has suffered before coming to me, I'm filled with joy in knowing that soon I can share with that person the peace and love that only Jesus can give.

And finally, I'm deeply touched by the faith and trust a penitent puts in me when he or she comes to confess. It's such a privilege to be able to share so intimately in another person's life, to be trusted with things perhaps no other human being on earth will ever be told. On so many occasions I have wanted to reach out and hug penitents, reassuring them that Jesus still loves them and that I don't think any less of them because of what they've told me. On a number of occasions I have done just that and the experience has been indescribably beautiful. People confess their sins to me in the sacrament of penance, but it is their goodness, their faith, their love that I remember.

In my forty-three years of priestly ministry I have had many joys, but none can begin to compare with the joy I feel when I share the Lord's forgiveness and peace with a penitent who has not known that peace for a long time. Some of the most exciting and thrilling moments of my life have been within the context of the sacrament of penance.

I remember sharing such thoughts with a group of high school students in one of my classes. One student, a tough football player, commented: "Gee, Father, you must lead a very dull life."

I was grateful for that comment, for it enabled me to share some of the more exciting moments of my life. One of my hobbies is snow and rock climbing. It is indeed a thrill to be standing on a ledge only two inches wide, four thousand feet up a vertical rock wall, while clinging to handholds half an inch wide and wondering how one will ever get out of such a predicament. There's nothing quite like it for excitement! Yet after such climbs I could fall asleep at night without too much difficulty.

I've gone after a bear with a sledgehammer and once charged a moose. I also happen to be a pilot and love to fly. I've made several emergency landings, twice after the landing gear malfunctioned. Talk about excitement! There isn't much more one could do for an encore. But after these experiences I was able to fall asleep at night within a reasonable length of time.

But what a thrill it is to share with penitents the peace of Jesus, to reassure them that it's okay, that He still loves them and in fact always has. After such wonderful and beautiful experiences, my joy is so intense that sleep is often impossible. I can appreciate the truth of the words of Jesus when he says: "I tell you, there will likewise be more joy in heaven over one repentant sinner than over ninety-nine righteous people who have no need to repent" (Luke 15:7).

The sacrament of penance is not just for those who have seriously turned away from God. By far the great majority of people who receive the sacrament are very good people, people who are striving to pattern their lives after the life and example of Jesus. So often as I minister of the sacrament of penance, I am deeply moved by their tremendous faith, their sorrow for their sins, and their desire to live a life of holiness.

They come to me, a priest, seeking spiritual direction and guidance, but often I feel that I should be the one seeking spiritual direction from them. They have already attained that degree of sanctity toward which I am still striving. The sincere manner in which they confess their sins, the fervor with which they pray the Act of Contrition, often brings tears to my eyes. How privileged I am to listen to them as they pour out their hearts to God! Such expressions of faith are a great source of inspiration and strength to me and challenge me to become a better priest.

For me it is no chore to "hear confessions." The many hours spent in the reconciliation room before Christmas and Easter and throughout the rest of the year are among the most enjoyable of my priestly ministry. We truly are privileged to be able to celebrate the fact that God loves us so much and is so willing, eager, and ready to forgive our sins. One of the greatest gifts we have as Catholics is the sacrament of penance, and the greatest privilege I have as a priest is that of trying to reflect the gentle, healing love of Jesus to sinners in need of reconciliation and forgiveness.

I had written an article reflecting on the joys I have experienced as a priest while administering the sacrament of reconciliation, which was published in the September 1980 issue of the *St. Anthony Messenger*. Seven years later on a particularly busy Sunday afternoon, just when I thought I could sit back and relax for several hours before late afternoon appointments and evening CCD classes with a group of high school students, the telephone began to ring incessantly, one call after another. I grumbled to myself as I got up to answer the phone for about the twentieth time, but remembering my penance, which I mentioned above, I tried to remain calm.

"Is this Father Mik-Kish?" some fellow asked, mispronouncing my name. When I assured him that I was, he asked if I was the priest who had written an article on the sacrament of penance some years ago. I suddenly was all ears; I had long since forgotten about the article and thus was flattered to think that someone still remembered it.

The caller went on to explain that he had read the article in 1980 and had carried it with him in his truck for three years, always intending to drop by to visit me while on a cross-country run. He sold his truck and apparently had left the article in it. After an extensive search in a local library, he managed to find the article and decided to call. He stated that he lived in the Chicago area, some six hundred miles away.

His next statement really floored me. He wanted to know if he could come to see me.

Not believing what I had just heard, I asked him to repeat where he was from. I then assured him that I would be happy to visit with him, but that I thought it was an awfully long way for him to drive. "Surely there are many priests in the Chicago area who would be glad to help you," I suggested, thinking that I could check the Official Catholic Directory and give him the names of several priests whom I know and who would receive him with compassion.

"Oh, I'm sure there are, Father," he replied, "but I don't know any of them. If it would be all right with you, I would prefer to drive out to see you."

Checking my schedule, we set a date for the following Tuesday at 7:00 p.m. I asked him for his name and phone number just in case some emergency should arise and I would have to reschedule our appointment. He told me his name was Bill and that he was calling from a phone booth. He obviously wanted to remain anonymous.

I hung up the receiver in disbelief! Someone wanted to drive six hundred miles just to receive the sacrament of reconciliation! Then I began to have doubts. What if he were some kind of a weirdo out to get me, or maybe he was some kind of a gangster! No one had ever confessed murder to me before. If he did commit murder, would I just absolve him or would I encourage him to turn himself over to the law? All such thoughts began to enter my mind.

I must confess that I was a bit apprehensive. I even asked a friend to drive by the rectory on Tuesday evening shortly after 7:00 p.m., to get the license number of the car that would be parked there. Just in case something did happen to me, I didn't want the offender to get away undetected.

Bill called again on Tuesday afternoon around 1:00 p.m., shortly after arriving in a nearby town. He wanted to know if he could come earlier since he had arrived hours ahead of schedule. I told him I would be free at 3:30 p.m. His polite manner convinced me that he meant no harm.

When he arrived promptly at 3:30 p.m., I greeted him at the door and invited him in. We visited for a few minutes; then he began to tell his story. It was so difficult and painful for him. He told me that even after driving six hundred miles he nearly chickened out and turned back when he arrived in town.

As is so often the case when hearing confessions, as he poured out his badness, his sinfulness, I could only marvel at his faith, his goodness, and his obvious love for God. He wasn't a gangster or murderer, nor was he notoriously evil. As a matter of fact, his sins were not so extraordinarily unusual, although he considered them to be the most heinous ever committed.

What a joy it was for me to share with him the "Good News" of God's love and forgiveness. There were tears of joy in my eyes and compassion in my heart as I prayed with him and gave him absolution.

We visited briefly after we had celebrated the sacrament before he got up to leave. "Tomorrow," he said, "I will receive Holy Communion for the first time in fourteen years." Through all these years he had faithfully attended Mass each Sunday, but had stayed away from receiving the sacraments.

"Would you like to receive now?" I asked.

"Oh, please! Could I?" he replied weakly with a faint smile.

Together we went over to church, prayed for a few minutes, and then I gave him the Holy Communion. What a beautiful way to conclude this celebration of reconciliation and peace!

Still not convinced that he had really driven six hundred miles to see me, I walked with him to his car and caught a glimpse of the license plate. Sure enough, they were Illinois plates. I offered to take him out to dinner before he headed back, but he stated simply that he wanted to put as many miles behind him as he could before dark. He planned to drive straight through the night.

As I reflected back upon this experience, I felt such a sense of joy in knowing that I was able to help this troubled soul find peace with God again after so many years of guilt and alienation. I still am filled with disbelief to think that someone actually made a round trip of 1,200 miles just to see me to receive the sacrament of reconciliation. At the same time I am also filled with a deep sense of sadness to think that this man chose to drive so far to see me when there are so many priests right in his own neighborhood who could have shared the Lord's forgiveness with him and given him better spiritual advice than I did.

Why didn't he go to one of them? Obviously he wanted to remain anonymous. I'm sure he was also afraid. He apparently had been touched by some of the things I had written in my article—the compassion I felt for sinners, the fact that I would never scold or condemn someone who came to me with sincere sorrow.

It is apparent to me that we priests need to share such thoughts with our people more often in our homilies. We need to let people know that we too are sinners and that we also find it difficult to approach a brother priest to confess our sins and seek forgiveness. We need to reflect on these words taken from the letter to the Hebrews (5:1-3):

Every high priest is taken from among men and made their representative before God, to offer gifts and sacrifices for sin. He is able to deal patiently with erring sinners, for he himself is beset by weakness and so must make sin offerings for himself as well as for the people.

Because we too are sinners, we need to be compassionate with sinners.

Unfortunately, even today when the church speaks of "celebrating" the sacrament of reconciliation, placing emphasis not so much on our "confessing" as on God's forgiveness, one still hears horror stories from penitents who were soundly scolded by a confessor and left the reconciliation room with little sense of having been reconciled with the Father.

Years ago when I first read about the waters at Meribah in the book of Numbers (20:7-13), I could not understand why God punished Moses for striking the rock in anger. I felt sorry for poor Moses. His people were so lacking in faith. In spite of all the great and wonderful saving deeds Yahweh had performed on behalf of His people, they continued to grumble and complain.

Had I been in Moses's shoes I just might have used that staff to bash their heads and not the rock!

It was only years later that I came to realize the reason why God was so displeased with Moses. By showing his anger, Moses had placed an obstacle between God and His people. In spite of their lack of faith, and their grumbling and complaining, once again God wanted to show His never-ending love for them by providing water in the parched wasteland. Moses in his anger had become an obstacle obstructing the love of God for His people.

Sometimes I wonder whether we priests also become obstacles between God and His people. We feel a compulsion to lecture and to scold sinners rather than to share with them the "Good News" of God's unconditional love, mercy, and forgiveness.

A teenager who has just dented the fender of the family car doesn't need a lecture on careful driving when he gets home; what he really needs just then is Mom's and Dad's compassionate understanding. Repentant sinners don't need lectures; they need God's loving acceptance and forgiveness.

If ever there was a perfect time for a lecture, it would have been the time when the woman who had been caught in the act of adultery was brought to Jesus. After Jesus dismissed the crowd, He could have said, "Look here, woman! You just came within an inch of losing your life. Don't you think it's time you shape up?"

Instead Jesus said, "Woman, where did they all disappear to? Has no one condemned you?"

"No one, sir," she answered.

Jesus said, "Nor do I condemn you. You may go. But from now on, avoid this sin" (John 8:10-11).

A friend once told me about the greatest job he had ever had. While attending college he worked part time for a florist, delivering flowers. What he liked so much about the job was the fact that every time he knocked on a door to make a delivery, he was greeted with a look of surprise, smiles, joy, and gratitude. He said, "I didn't have to do anything. I just delivered the flowers and was privileged to share in all the joy and gratitude that followed."

We priests are in a similar situation. When we administer the sacrament of reconciliation, we are in the privileged position of sharing the "Good News" of God's infinite love, mercy, and forgiveness with sinners. It doesn't cost us anything; we're just the privileged ones who get to share in the joy of the penitent. Perhaps we need to spend a little more time reflecting upon this.

The fact that a troubled soul would make a journey of 1,200 miles to receive the sacrament of reconciliation from a priest who expressed his feelings of compassion for sinners convinces me that we priests need to express such thoughts more often. We need to assure people that we will be empathetic and compassionate with repentant sinners, for we too are sinners. We need to reassure them that our primary purpose as confessors is to share God's forgiveness and peace with them and not to scold, chastise, or condemn. We need to assure them that we will not become stumbling blocks or obstacles in the way of God's mercy, and we need to act accordingly. Once people truly begin to experience "reconciliation" in this sacrament, we will no longer have to worry about the decline in numbers who receive this sacrament.

THE INFLUENCE OF PARENTS

MANY TIMES OVER the years I have been asked: "Why did you decide to become a priest?"

Quite frankly, I find this a difficult question to answer. Some of my classmates had very clear and definite reasons for wanting to become priests, whereas I had no ready response to that question. I wanted to do something worthwhile with my life. Helping people on their journey through life on their way to eternity is perhaps the best reason I can offer today, but when I first entered the seminary, I could not have given any profound reason for wanting to become a priest. Perhaps the idea was instilled in me by my parents, two faith-filled individuals who were of the belief that the greatest blessing that could be bestowed upon a family was that of having a child choose a vocation to the priesthood or religious life.

My mother and dad were both so deeply religious. For them faith and life were so intertwined that it would have been impossible to have one without the other. A conversation about any topic could be turned into a religious lesson so naturally that we children didn't even realize it. It was only some years after I had been ordained that I became aware of this.

One day, when I was at home on my day off, I was sitting in the living room reading a magazine when my mother and little niece came into the house, carrying armfuls of freshly cut flowers. As they were busily arranging them into bouquets on the kitchen table, I overheard the following conversation, which was initiated by my niece with all the enthusiasm of a seven-year-old:

"I like flowers more than I like trees!" she said.

"Oh, I don't! I like trees more than I like flowers," my mother replied. "Trees give us their wood to build our homes. Trees give us firewood to warm our homes in winter. They shade us from the hot sun in summer and shelter us from the cold winds in winter. Trees give us such beautiful autumn colors."

By this time I was totally engrossed in the conversation and surprised at the many benefits of trees my mother was giving. She continued: "And there is one more thing I like about trees. Whenever I see a tree, I think of the tree of the cross. God loves us so much that He sent His Son Jesus to die on the cross for us."

There was a pause; then I heard my niece say, "Gee, I never thought of that!"

Suddenly I realized that my mother and I had many similar such conversations as I was growing up. Whatever the subject might have been, both Mom and Dad could turn it into a religious lesson so naturally that we children didn't even realize it. God was such a part of our upbringing that it was only natural to include Him in our daily conversations. I have no doubt whatsoever that my mother did think of the tree of the cross whenever she saw a tree, so much was her faith part of her daily life.

And so it was with Dad! Like most small farmers, when I was growing up, we had a few acres of pastureland on which a few herds of milk cows grazed. I can remember many an evening walking out into the pasture to bring the cows home at milking time. As dad and I walked along, a full moon might be rising or a sunset was particularly beautiful, prompting Dad to say, "Isn't that a beautiful full moon!" or "Isn't that a beautiful sunset! God is so good to give us such a beautiful world in which to live!"

Two very simple statements, but what an impact they have had on my life. I am so keenly aware of the beauty of nature around me. I love the outdoors! I notice every sunrise and sunset; I love the mountains! My idea of a vacation is to backpack in the backcountry or go rock climbing in the Tetons or Rocky Mountain National Park, spending a night on a ledge half way up a rock wall, and all the while praising and thanking God for the beauty of His creation.

When I was ordained to priesthood, I chose for my memorial card a mountain scene, with a quote from the book of Wisdom: "From the beauty of created things comes a corresponding perception of the beauty of the Creator" (Ws 13:5).

Every day as I enjoy the beauty of the world around me and express my gratitude to God for the gift of His creation, I also thank God for my dad who helped me become aware of the beauty of creation and see it as God's special gift.

FATHER JOSEPH A. MIKSCH

MY FATHER'S BLESSING

I ALSO TREASURE another precious gift my dad gave me: the gift of his fatherly blessing. The day I left home for the seminary was a difficult day for me. Leaving home for the first time is never easy, especially when one is so young as I was. The seminary was 250 miles from home, so I wouldn't be coming home until Christmas vacation.

The car was already packed. I knew I had everything I needed, but I wasn't ready to leave just yet, so I went back to the house and walked through each room to make sure I wasn't leaving anything behind. Dad was standing by the front door. Now as I look back, I wonder what he was thinking as he watched his youngest child prepare to leave the nest.

When I was finally ready to leave, Dad said to me, "Joe, kneel down! I will give you my fatherly blessing!"

I had never heard of such a thing. Priests and bishops gave blessings, but parents?

Obediently I knelt down. Dad placed his hand on my head and prayed that if God wanted me to become a priest, that I would persevere in my studies (Dad knew how much I hated school). He also prayed that if I became a priest, that I would be a good priest. Then he made the sign of the cross over me, extended his hands to me, and helped me up. As he did so, he said, "Joe, I hope someday you will give this blessing back to me as my priest son!"

Twelve years later, with hands still wet with sacred chrism, I can't begin to describe the joy I felt as I walked down from the altar and gave my dad and mother my first priestly blessing!

I have since been blessed by cardinals and archbishops, and once even by the pope, but no blessing will ever mean as much to me as the blessing given to me by my father.

At the beginning of the Rite of the Baptism of Infants, one of the first things the priest does is trace the sign of the cross on the infant's forehead as he says, "(Child's name), the Christian community welcomes you with great joy. In its name I sign you with the sign of the cross and invite your parents and godparents to do the same." I also invite big brothers and sisters to do the same, after which I say to them, "Do you realize what you just did? You just blessed your little brother (or sister)! That means you can never fight with him (or her)!"

I encourage parents to bless their children often. Bless them when you put them to bed at night, when they go off to that first day of preschool, kindergarten, junior high. These can be special moments in their lives.

Some parents who have been doing this have told me that as their children are growing up, they also want to bless Mom and Dad before they go to bed.

I also encourage engaged couples and married couples to bless each other, tracing the sign of the cross on each other's forehead and asking God's blessing upon this person who is so special and so dear.

FATHER'S DAY LETTER

SOME WEEKS AFTER we buried his father, who had died suddenly at the age of fifty-five, a young man came to me for grief counseling. As we talked for several hours during the course of the next few weeks, the regret I heard the young man express most often was the fact that he had never told his dad how much he loved him. His was a very close-knit family; they showed their love in many ways, but never expressed that love verbally. As a result of our conversations, on a number of occasions in my homilies I expressed the fact that we need to tell our loved ones that we love them.

Some months later as Father's Day was drawing near, I realized that I needed to practice what I was preaching. I too came from a family in which we never doubted our love for one another, but we never expressed that love verbally. I had gotten a beautiful Father's Day card for Dad, along with a box of candy—I always bought Dad candy for Father's Day, knowing that he would share it with the rest of us! But this year, instead of just signing the card, I wrote Dad a letter in which I told him how much I loved him and how I respected him and looked up to him as a man of faith.

Dad was always very proud of me, his priest son. Nothing delighted him more than when I would come home on my day off and would be working in the field. A salesman or stranger might drive up and stop to talk to Dad about some business, and Dad would delight in introducing me as his priest son.

In my letter I told Dad that I knew he was proud of me because I was a priest, but also expressed the fact that I felt very much like a little child when I stood beside him and my mother as a person of faith.

I felt very good about the letter I had written and couldn't wait to give it to Dad. On Father's Day I drove home in the afternoon and presented Dad with my card, letter, and gift. Dad read the card and letter, standing right in front of me, unwrapped the box of candy, then just looked at me, and said, "Thank you, Joe!"

That was it! I remember driving back to the rectory that night feeling rather disappointed. I had just poured my heart out and had told Dad the most important thing I had ever told him, and all he could say was "Thank-you."

It wasn't until months later that I came to realize how much my letter meant to Dad. Late in October I went home one Sunday afternoon for some kind of family gathering. The house was filled with relatives and neighbors. I was visiting in the living room, and Dad was sitting at the kitchen table visiting with others. Suddenly he got up and left the room. When he returned, I noticed he was carrying a box, which he kept in our family safe and in which he kept his most important papers. My curiosity was roused. I couldn't imagine what papers Dad was going to share with our guests. When he pulled out a certain envelope, I realized he was sharing my Father's Day card and letter with our guests. It meant so much to him that he kept it with his most important papers in our family safe. That night, as I drove back to my parish, I felt such joy as I knew how much my letter meant to dad.

The following year as Father's Day drew near, the last that Dad was to be with us, I again wrote him a letter, telling him that I loved him and that I was proud of him as my dad and as a man of deep faith. Again, when I presented my card, letter, and box of candy to him on Father's Day, he read the card and letter, looked at me, and said, "Thank you, Joe!" This time I didn't mind that this was all he said because I knew how much he appreciated the card and letter.

Later that afternoon Dad and I took a walk around the farmyard. As we were strolling along, Dad suddenly stopped and said to me, "Joe, I really appreciate your card and letter. Because you said the things you said, there are some things I would like to share with you." He then went on to tell me how proud he was of me, my brother, and sisters. He told me how grateful he was to God for the blessing of a good life. As a young man he was very sickly and as a result didn't do much farming like his older brothers. He stayed more in the house and did household chores. Thus, when he married, he wasn't sure he would succeed as a farmer. He was thus so grateful to God that he had been able to provide a good life for his family. Most important, he was thankful to God for a dear and loving wife and mother for his children.

It was a conversation that I will never forget, nor was it the last such conversation we had. Now the doors were open, and Dad and I could share more deeply than we ever had before. We had our last such conversation the afternoon before Dad died.

FATHER JOSEPH A. MIKSCH

I had taken an afternoon off to take my mother and dad to town to do some shopping. While Mother was still shopping, Dad and I were sitting in the car. Dad initiated the conversation by stating that at the age of eighty he knew he didn't have many more years on this earth. He wasn't afraid of dying; he was at peace with God, having done his best to live a good life. The only thing he feared was a disabling illness like a stroke. He dreaded the thought of going to a nursing home or of being a burden to the family. Then he added, "A heart attack wouldn't be that bad."

Little did I realize that within less than twenty-four hours God would grant Dad his wish. My sister called the next afternoon to tell me that Dad had just had a heart attack and was being rushed to the hospital by ambulance. By the time I arrived at the hospital, Dad had already expired.

While it was extremely difficult for me to officiate at his funeral and preach the homily, I felt an inner joy and peace in knowing that Dad had gotten his wish and that he was safely at home with the Lord.

How grateful I am that I wrote those letters to Dad on Father's Day. What a difference they made in both of our lives. I shared that story in my homily and urged all present to express their love to their loved ones. At the Sign of Peace when I went to greet my mother, sisters, and brother, my brother embraced me and said, "Joe, I love you!"

I always loved my brother and knew he loved me, but I can't begin to tell you how much hearing him say those words meant to me. Ever since that moment I have felt differently toward my brother. What power those three words "I love you" have!

JUST HOPING YOU WOULDN'T MAKE
A FOOL OF YOURSELF

THE FACT THAT I was their priest son was a cause for great joy and a sense of pride for my deeply religious, faith-filled parents. I also caused them much worry and, at times, embarrassment because of the foolish things I did.

While in college and the first three years I was studying theology, I spent my summers working as a park employee for the Department of the Interior in Grand Teton National Park. Along with thirty-one others, I spent my summers working to maintain some three hundred miles of hiking trails which led through the park. What an incredible way to spend a summer! It was like being paid to be on a vacation.

I spent one entire summer living in a tent. I let my hair grow and didn't shave, thus by the end of summer I truly looked like a mountain man. At the end of summer I took the bus home. Although the bus was crowded, I had the last five seats in the rear of the bus to myself. No one else cared to sit by me. Admittedly I did look a little grubby!

When the bus pulled into the station near my home town, I saw Mom and Dad standing outside, waiting to pick me up. Not sure if they would recognize me, I decided to play a little trick on them. The last one off the bus, I walked right past them and stepped inside the bus station. Mom and Dad just stood there, waiting for me to get off the bus. When no one else got off the bus, they stood there for a minute or two before entering the station. After a minute or two, Dad said to Mom, looking toward me: "You don't suppose that's Joe, do you?"

They came over and claimed me, but the following weekend my mother insisted that I attend Mass at a neighboring parish where people wouldn't recognize me. Once I shaved and got a haircut, I was allowed to attend Mass in my home parish.

Apparently Mom didn't have much confidence in me! I guess she knew me all too well. On one occasion some years after I had been ordained, I was asked to give the keynote address at a fund raising dinner for a major campaign. I had worked long and hard on my presentation and had some nice things to say about the two teachers, my parents, who had the greatest influence on my life as a man of faith, so I invited my mother to attend.

My presentation went very well and was well received by everyone at the banquet. Later that evening as I was taking my mother home, I expected her to say something to me about my talk, but she didn't say a word. Finally, I asked her: "Mom, what did you think of my talk?"

Without a moment's hesitation she replied, "Oh! I didn't hear a word you said. I was just praying so you wouldn't make a fool of yourself!"

JESUS TOUCHED ME

O NE OF THE special privileges of being a priest is that of being mistakenly identified as God or Jesus.

As pastor of a parish in a small town in Nebraska, a community of about four hundred people with nearly as many stray cats and dogs, one blinking yellow traffic light and a few stop signs, I often walked the three blocks from the rectory to the post office. One afternoon as I was walking downtown, a mother drove up and parked in front of the post office; she quickly darted inside, leaving her children in the car. A little boy in the back seat, a lad of about three, frantically rolled down the window and began shouting excitedly, waving to me when I was still a half block away: "Hi, God! Hi, God!"

Grooming my hair has never been an important priority in my life. When students in the Catholic High School where I taught commented on my unkempt hair, I would tell them that I spend twenty seconds in front of the mirror each morning. If my hair isn't groomed by then, too bad! I won't have to look at it for the rest of the day, so why bother? Admittedly my hair does become rather unsightly at times. One mother once informed me that even the four-year-olds had noticed. Shortly after I had gotten a haircut, her son came home from church and announced, "Mom! Mom! God finally got a haircut!"

At weekend liturgies I used to walk down the aisle at the Sign of Peace to greet the people who are standing near the end of the pews. The small children were always eager to reach out to shake my hand—well, most of the time they are eager to do so. I remember one little girl standing next to her dad near the center aisle with a purse slung over her right arm. After I shook hands with her dad, I reached over to shake her little hand. Apparently she thought I was going to steal her purse; she stepped back and clung to that purse with both hands. Obviously she had heard too many money talks and was in no mood to give any more.

On another occasion as I walked down the aisle greeting people, I greeted a mother who was holding her little three-year-old daughter. I reached out and grasped her tiny hand with my index finger and shook it. Her face became one radiant smile. As I walked back up the aisle, I heard her say repeatedly, "Mommy, Jesus touched me! Jesus touched me!"

It's easy to understand why little children become confused and think that the priest is God or Jesus. Their mothers and dads tell them over and over again that they are going to God's house to see Jesus. They look at pictures of Jesus with His long, flowing robes in their children's Bibles, and then see the priest who is dressed in similar long, flowing vestments.

Often when parents come forward to receive Holy Communion, their little children will walk up with them and gaze up at me. I sometimes wonder what is going through their minds at such moments. Nearly six feet two inches tall, standing on a step while distributing Holy Communion, to those little tots standing there with their heads tilted way back to look up at me, I must indeed appear to be as tall as God. No wonder they become confused and mistakenly identify me as God or Jesus.

While I smile when the little ones call me God or Jesus and am flattered by the compliment—after all, one can receive no greater compliment—I am also profoundly touched. At such moments I realize what a tremendous responsibility I have as a priest to try to reflect the love of God and Jesus to all people. People do come to me hoping to experience the love of Jesus, His acceptance, His forgiveness, His consolation, and His peace.

When there is no one else to turn to, people turn to their priests. Those who do not feel that they are accepted by others often cling to their priests. The brokenhearted, those experiencing a difficult crisis, the sick and the suffering, and those who have discovered that the world in which they live has no answers to their problems often turn to their priests to find support, meaning, and purpose to their lives. They turn to their priests to experience the healing touch of Jesus, to find that peace which only He can give.

In his second letter to the Corinthians, St. Paul states, "We are ambassadors for Christ, God as it were appealing through us" (2 Cor. 5:20). As I walked back up the aisle after greeting that little girl and heard her say excitedly: "Mommy, Jesus touched me!" Paul's words took on a new meaning for me. I am called to be an "ambassador for Christ," and I realize now more than ever that I must live my life in such a way and minister to my people in such a way that they too can walk away saying, "Jesus touched me!"

As I reflect back upon that experience, I also have come to realize that through the innocence of that little child "Jesus touched me!"

VISITING ELDERLY PARISHIONERS

O NE OF THE more enjoyable duties and privileges, which a priest has, is that of visiting the elderly shut-ins in the parish and bringing them Holy Communion. For many of them a visit by their pastor is truly the highlight of their week. Such visits can lead to deep and treasured friendships, and also to some rather interesting and humorous experiences.

I think of Barbara, for example. Although she was in her nineties, she still was mentally alert; with a twinkle in her eyes she loved to recall some of the mischievous things her children had done in their youth, much to their embarrassment.

She also had a very mean dog! I never got out of my car until I was sure that the dog was either tied up in the yard or locked in the washroom near the entrance of her home. Even her own grandchildren were not above suspicion in the eyes of this vicious mutt. Whenever I would mention her dog, she would smile and beam with delight: "Oh, Father, he's such a good dog! He's a good dog, Father!" she would say.

He was a good dog, a good watchdog, and that gave her a sense of security and companionship. No bum, stranger, not ever her parish priest, would dare set foot on the place while that dog was on the loose.

Once when I arrived, I got out of the car and cautiously walked toward the door, carefully looking around to make sure the dog was nowhere in the yard. The woman's daughter met me at the front door and apologetically explained to me that I could not come in. The dog was on the loose in the house and she had not been able to corner it to lock it in the washroom. Would I mind if I met her mother in the washroom?

She escorted me to the washroom, closed the door lest the dog sees me there, and then ushered her mother out to meet me. Her mother sat on a chair while I leaned back against the washing machine. While saying the Communion prayers, I was interrupted several times as she reassured me that "he was a good dog."

There was another couple whom I would visit regularly. He was nearly blind and bedfast for the last seven years of his life. His wife was constantly at his side, ministering to his every need. The first time I visited this couple, having just arrived in the parish, I prayed with them and gave them Holy Communion. Afterward she asked me if I would care for a "cup of coffee."

I learned that a "cup of coffee" consisted of three eggs, half a pound of bacon, a stack of toast, fruit, coffee, and a jigger of Southern Comfort. Although I've never been one to have a nip for breakfast, she insisted that a little drink would be good for me. After that first visit I also learned to wait until I was ready to leave before drinking the Southern Comfort. Being such a hospitable person, as soon as one took a sip, she was there with the bottle to refill the glass.

For some unknown reason, after visiting this couple I always felt extremely relaxed throughout the rest of the morning.

When I was transferred to another parish, the priest who took my place was treated with similar kindness. I should have warned him not to drink his "juice" until he was ready to leave, since this woman was in the habit of refilling your glass whenever you weren't looking. After his first visit and "cup of coffee," and the equivalent of four jiggers of Apricot Brandy, he went to school to teach his morning classes. Midway through the class period the principal heard a lot of noise and laughter coming from his normally quiet and disciplined classroom. Upon investigating, she found him slumped over his desk, fast asleep, much to the delight of his students. She knew immediately that Father had been on his morning Communion calls.

Each parishioner or family has its own unique style, or ritual, when Father comes. One elderly woman always insisted that I have a cup of coffee, a sweet roll, and a glass of wine with her after she had received Holy Communion. She had a special glass for me, a rather large one too. A third of the way from the bottom was a red line with the inscription "For Women." Two thirds of the way up was another line "For Men." At the very top was a third line with the inscription, "For Hogs." Every Sunday she would set the glass before me and fill it to the brim.

Since I had to drive a few miles through the country and cross a long, narrow one-lane bridge to get back to the rectory, I would always wait until I was ready to leave before drinking the wine, and then would try to get across the bridge before my vision became blurred and I would see two bridges.

Visiting shut-ins can also be dangerous! On one occasion I was viciously attacked by three tame Canadian geese. With wings flapping, they came fluttering and hissing after me, pecking away at my arms and legs as I ran for the safety of the house. I've had experience in dealing with mean dogs, but no one had ever told me how to deal with these creatures. I received little comfort or assistance from the old-timer, who was standing on the porch; he hadn't seen such a comic scene in years and was thoroughly enjoying it.

Then there was Albrecht, nearly ninety years old and nearly deaf. I don't think he ever understood a word I said, so when I came to visit him I said very little. I would greet him, shake his hand, then sit in a rocking chair, and listen for half an hour as he told me his life's story. It was always the same. In fact, I used to play little games when I would visit Albrecht. I would check my watch when I sat down and would say to myself: "At one thirty he will be telling me about his son who was in the army." Sure enough, at one thirty he would be at that part of his story.

On other occasions I would try to predict what would come next in his story. Sometimes I could recite verbatim what he was going to tell me.

After visiting Albrecht several times a month for three years, I discovered just how much my visits meant to him. One day another elderly gentleman came up to me and told me that he had a compliment for me. He had been visiting with Albrecht (I wondered how he could since Albrecht never heard a word I said). He told me that Albrecht had said, "You know, I really enjoy it when Father Joe comes to visit. He is such an interesting fellow to talk to."

I really chuckled when I heard that, but I realized then how important it was for him to tell and retell his life's story. By listening to him I was affirming him and assuring him that his life had been worth living and that he was important.

I'm sure every priest who has gone on Communion calls could share similar stories. There is even the story, I'm sure it is just that, of a priest who dropped by to visit an elderly couple. While sitting around the kitchen table he began to help himself to some peanuts in a dish in the center of the table. Suddenly he realized that he had just eaten the last peanut. He felt rather foolish for eating all of them, so he began to apologize. The elderly gentleman immediately tried to put him at ease. "Oh, Father," he said, "don't worry about that. You know, at our age my wife's and my teeth aren't so good. We can't chew the peanuts anymore, so we just suck the chocolate off them."

I no longer eat peanuts when visiting the elderly.

FATHER JOSEPH A. MIKSCH

PANHANDLERS

SEVERAL DAYS AFTER arriving at my first priestly assignment, I had my first encounter with a bum asking for a handout. He gave a heart-wrenching story about how he had been wounded in the Korean conflict and needed bus fare to get to the VA Hospital in North Dakota and money for food. Filled with compassion, I fell for his story hook, line, and sinker, reached for my wallet, and gave him $10. Ten dollars may not seem like a lot today, but back then I was only receiving a stipend of $75 per month.

That evening at the dinner table the pastor asked me what the gentleman at the door wanted. When I retold the man's story and told him how much I had given, the pastor lectured me for half an hour, informing me that I had been taken. Experience was to verify what my pastor told me.

I wonder how many stories I have heard over the years from "veterans" going from Texas to North Dakota to check into the VA Hospital. There must be a lot of VA hospitals in North Dakota. I've learned too that veterans never have any identification papers, no family or friends, and no way of ever verifying their stories. Even when they have "just been dismissed from the hospital," one cannot call that hospital to verify that they had been there.

Some of the more sophisticated folks who come to the door drive their own vehicles. They need gas money, usually to visit someone who is dying somewhere far away; they have left their jobs in Arizona to be with their sick friend in Wisconsin. One such fellow told me his sad story and wanted money for gas. There was a gas station just across the street from the rectory, so I told him to drive over and I would top off his tank. With that, he began to stammer and stutter, but I insisted that he drive over and pull up to the pump. I put the nozzle into the gas tank. The pump scarcely began to pump when the tank was full. The bill came to seventeen cents!

One poor fellow came to the rectory door one chilly autumn day. I fixed a ham and cheese sandwich and gave him a can of Pepsi. He looked rather cold, so I gave him a bright red parka, which I no longer needed. Some time later the county sheriff dropped by with several wanted posters and asked if per chance I might have seen either of those men.

I told the officer in reply, pointing to the picture on one of the posters: "You won't have a difficult time spotting him! He's wearing a bright red parka!" Several hours later he was picked up by the police in a nearby town.

Professional panhandlers know the best time to strike is when the priest is busy. A good time to catch a priest is shortly before Mass, although that doesn't always work. Experience has taught me to tell such individuals that I will be available after Mass. If they expect a handout, they will have to spend some time in church praying that I will be generous.

I learned this the hard way. One fellow came up right before Mass, asking for some money for food. Normally I prefer not to give anyone money, so on this occasion I decided to play it cool. I called the local restaurant and told them I was sending a man down for a meal; I would be down after Mass to pay for it.

Later, when I went down to the café to pay, I was shocked when I was presented with a $16 bill. It seems this bum had expensive tastes and ordered the largest prime rib. I paid the bill, but I made it known that in future such people get hamburger. That's what I eat; that's what they can eat!

What really added fuel to the fire was the fact that this fellow had money to buy cigarettes and several beers to go with his meal.

Really clever people have other ways of getting money from you quickly. When one lady came to the door, I invited her into my office and was prepared to listen to her story. She began by telling me she had this rare disease; then she suddenly jumped up and began to apologize, saying she had wet my chair. I quickly gave her $20 just to get her out and then spent the rest of the morning sanitizing my office.

I remember when I was in the seminary several priests who had been ordained only a year or two earlier came back to share stories of some of their experiences. One was quite a humorous fellow who had many good stories to relate. One thing he said that caught my attention was this: "Even if you know someone is giving you a line, sometimes a good story is worth a few bucks!"

I've always remembered that and have given individuals a few bucks simply because they had an original story. If I have time, I love to sit and visit for a long time, ask a lot of questions, and make the individual work for a handout.

Recently I had a fellow stop by with a truly unique story. He told me he worked for a firm in St. Louis that bought and sold used aircraft. He had a briefcase filled with pictures of twin engine aircraft with price tags ranging from $250,000 to $500,000. He was spending a few days in our community, looking around to see if any such planes were available. He needed money for a hotel room.

Now one would think that if you worked for a company that bought and sold airplanes costing up to half a million dollars, you would have some kind of travel allowance for food and overnight accommodations, so it didn't take a genius to figure out that he was a phony. I also happen to be a pilot and know something about aircraft and electronics, so I decided to have some fun.

First, I asked him all kinds of questions about the performance data of some of the aircraft pictures he showed me. Soon he was stammering and stuttering, making excuses as to why he didn't know the specifics on each aircraft. Now I don't know an awful lot about airplanes, but having flown single engine aircraft for nearly forty years, I can give you a very close estimate on a plane's performance capabilities.

It became even more interesting when I began to ask him about the electronics aboard these aircraft. He didn't have a clue as to what I was talking about, so I finally said to him, "Your story really isn't very credible! Could I have the phone number of your corporate office in St. Louis? I'd like to check out your story!"

With that he became unglued. He jumped up and yelled at me: "Are you calling me a liar?"

"No," I replied. "It's just that I don't find your story very credible!"

With that he threw his pictures of airplanes back into his briefcase and headed for the door, stopping before exiting to tell me that he was going to sue me for calling him a liar. Thus far, I haven't received a subpoena, summoning me to appear in court!

I felt bad that the poor fellow left on such a note. I was prepared to give him a gift card for some food at a local grocery store for his original approach.

Another approach that has been tried several times on me and other priests is this: On a Friday evening around 6:00 p.m. someone would call, identifying himself as a member of our community or parish. "You remember me, don't you, Father? I just talked to you after Mass last Sunday." Then he would proceed to tell me that his car had just broken down in a distant town, the mechanic wanted $400 up front to fix it, his folks were out of town, and he didn't have any money. Would I wire $400 to him?

If it truly were a parishioner that I knew, I probably would wire him some money, but I wouldn't wire money to someone whose name I didn't recognize even if he did talk to me after Mass. Furthermore, I talk to so many people after each Mass on Sunday that I wouldn't recall talking with many of them.

Once when I received such a call, I asked the fellow where he lived and what his address was. The address he gave me would have put him right in the middle of the Platte River.

On another such attempt, I asked the caller, who told me he had talked to me after Mass, how many steeples our church had. After a long pause, he replied that he really didn't know. Our church has no steeple, just one long, flat roof. Sorry! I wasn't able to help either of these callers!

I have been taken for a fool on a few occasions, perhaps more often that I care to admit. One person gave me a sob story about how her parents had kicked her out of her home; she had no place to go and needed a place to stay overnight. I ended up providing her with a motel room, only to learn next day from the manager that she had hosted a wild drug and alcohol party for her friends that night.

There are times when people truly are hard up and need a helping hand. On occasion I have given such individuals rides into a larger community where I could put them on a bus, or put them up for a night or two in a motel. I've fed people, taken them out to eat, I even let one individual live in the spare bedroom of the rectory for six weeks while he completed a course in nursing, which would enable him to get a job in a local nursing home.

Most priests and ministers are more than willing to help people who are truly in need, but we hate to be taken by con artists.

Dealing with people at the door has also taught me many lessons in humility. I don't mind helping people who are truly in need, but sometimes I am selfish and chintzy in doling out my personal funds. Often when I have been tight and gave a mere fraction of what I could have afforded to give someone, I will receive a card in the mail with a generous gift for my personal use. On such occasions I find myself thinking: "How could I be so tight! Why didn't I give that person more!"

I have truly come to realize that God is never outdone in generosity. When we give our gifts away, He will repay us a hundredfold.

A man came to the rectory door to visit with one priest I know. His car had broken down, and he needed bus money to get somewhere. This particular priest was a man of tremendous compassion. Rather than give the fellow a few bucks to get a bus ticket, he offered to take him there.

The priest was driving an old clunker of a vehicle, a "prayer car," the kind you always have to pray that you will reach your destination. When he dropped the man off, he was very grateful.

Several weeks later at the annual parish bazaar, a new pickup truck was standing in the parking lot. The truck was a gift for the priest who had given the bum a ride. Apparently he was a rather wealthy man and wanted to show his appreciation and gratitude.

With this event in the back of my mind, I keep trying to be nice to people who come to the door in need! Perhaps if I had been more patient with the fellow with the airplane picture, I might be flying my own plane today.

Speaking of "prayer cars," I've been driving them for years! I used to become upset when my car would break down, but I've gradually come to the realization that such breakdowns can lead to some rather interesting adventures, after which I often have more stories to use in my homilies.

Late one night as I was driving home from a meeting, I learned the efficacious value of prayer. About thirty miles from home I heard a loud explosion. Looking in the rearview mirror, I saw a ball of fire behind the car. I thought the muffler had blown up; the engine was so loud, it sounded like a tractor engine with a straight exhaust pipe. I didn't mind the noise so much, but every few minutes the motor would begin to sputter, and I was afraid it was going to die. It definitely was time to pray.

My prayers seemed to be answered. Every time the motor would begin to sputter, I would pray, and it would run smoothly again. It was so noisy, however, that I realized I couldn't take the normal route home through a large town. I would have been arrested for disturbing the peace, so I took a roundabout way home. Four or five times I thought the motor was going to die, but each time, after a fervent prayer, it would catch again and run smoothly. At 1:00 a.m. I pulled into the garage, breathing a sigh of relief and thanking God for getting me home safely.

Next morning after Mass I headed down to the local garage to have the mechanic look at my sick, noisy vehicle. It stalled right in front of the post office and wouldn't start. The garage was just across the street. The mechanic was walking across the street to get his mail. I rolled down the window, but before I could say anything, he said to me: "Just leave it, Father Joe. I'll push it in!"

God often exceeds my expectations when it comes to answering my prayers!

SURVIVAL

ONE MIGHT THINK that a chapter with such a title, by one who used to spend his summers camping out in the backcountry of our national parks and spent his time rock climbing and flying airplanes, might be about surviving in the wilderness after an accident or plane crash. Not so! When I think of surviving, I think back on how I survived seminary life! One of the reasons why I feel absolutely certain that God wanted me to become a priest is the fact that I survived the seminary.

Back in the late 1950s and early 1960s, life in the seminary was rather Spartan, extremely structured with strict discipline. By nature I am a rather free-spirited, fun-loving, and adventuresome sort of fellow. Thus, my days in the seminary were not the happiest of my life, nor was I the model seminarian. To my way of thinking, life in the seminary in those days was very similar to life in a state penitentiary, the only difference being that we had crosses on our turrets while the penitentiary had machine guns.

My experiences in the seminary, however, did help me come to a better understanding of the book of Judges in the Old Testament.

One sees a basic five-step pattern, which is repeated over and over in the book of Judges:

1. The Israelites sin and turn away from God.
2. Their enemy begins to oppress them.
3. They turn to God and beg for deliverance.
4. God sends a judge to free them from danger.
5. All goes well for a while until they stray again, and then the pattern repeats itself.

So it was for me in the seminary. All would be going well until I decided to break some rule or skip a class. Suddenly I would realize that I was about to get caught, I would pray to God for deliverance, and promise never to stray again. I would get by without having to face the consequences and within a few weeks would find myself in another such situation.

For example, every Saturday morning we would have an hour-long chant practice in preparation for Sunday's liturgy. To me nothing was more boring that singing Latin chants for an hour, so naturally I would skip. Never being one with great foresight, I would usually skip on the coldest day, thinking I would hide outside, but forgetting to take a jacket along. Realizing that I would soon freeze to death, I would have to risk sneaking back into the building and finding a place to hide until class was over.

On one particular day I concluded that the safest place to hide in a seminary would be in the women's restroom. It would seem logical to conclude that in an all-male Catholic seminary that would be the safest place to hide!

No sooner had I stepped inside than I heard the clomp, clomp, clomp of two women wearing high-heeled shoes coming toward the restroom. It was too late to get out, so I jumped into one of the stalls, closed the door, and panicked. Realizing that they would be able to see my shoes and black trousers, I jumped up on the stool and squatted there.

My heart jumped into my throat as one of the women tried to pull the stall door open, and then used the next one while the two conversed and wondered why the door behind which I was hiding was jammed. Now I have no idea what women do when they powder their noses, but I can tell you one thing: they certainly take a long time to do it. I didn't think they would ever leave and all the while I prayed with all the fervor of my heart: "Dear God, if I ever get out of this one, I will never skip chant class again!"

On another occasion when I did attend chant class, one of the seminarians fell asleep. A hammer had been left on the professor's stand (I think the custodian had left it there after repairing one of the pews). Picking up the hammer, the professor shook it toward the sleeping student. Much to his surprise and chagrin, the head of the hammer flew off and conked the poor student on the head. No major damage was done to the head of the hammer. The student had quite a lump on his forehead, but the poor professor nearly had a heart attack.

There were several stagnant lakes on campus, one of which was aptly named "Polio Pond." One afternoon three classmates built a raft consisting of four fifty-gallon drums tied together with several planks laid out on top. Late that night, long after curfew, they snuck out of the building and went sailing across the lake. For some reason the raft broke apart when they were out in the middle of the lake. Two fellows managed to swim to the shore, but the third fellow didn't make it.

The two survivors walked around the lake several times, not daring to call out too loudly for fear of being detected by some faculty member. Their friend was nowhere to be found. They could only conclude that he had drowned.

Not only was it a tragedy to have lost a classmate and friend, they also realized that if they reported to anyone what had happened, they could be expelled from the seminary. Remember, these were the days when discipline was strictly enforced, and violating evening curfew was considered a major breach of discipline!

After considerable discussion the two finally decided to sneak back into their building and act as if nothing had happened. After all, if their friend were dead, there was nothing they could do for him. There was no point in causing a great commotion and getting expelled in the process.

What an incredibly long night it was for them! On the few occasions that they did doze off, they had nightmares in which they saw their classmate's body rising and floating on the surface.

Next morning, before going to Mass, they walked around the lake but found no body. When they attended Mass and didn't see him there, they knew their worse fears were true, but they had sworn to keep his death a secret in order to avoid expulsion. After breakfast they went to his room, hoping against hope that he might be there.

Martha and Mary could not have been happier or more relieved at the resurrection of Lazarus than these two were when they found their friend in his room. When the raft broke up, he swam to the opposite shore. When the two had walked around the lake, he was too exhausted to call out to them, having barely made it to shore, so they walked by without seeing him and went to their rooms. He waited outside until it was quite late, and then snuck back to his room.

One year as Christmas was approaching, the faculty and student body had a Christmas party. Several of my classmates had gotten a bottle of Scotch to present to the faculty moderator who lived on our floor. They were trying to think of some novel way in which to present the gift to him.

We lived on the fourth floor of a five-storey building. Being an avid rock climber, I suggested that perhaps I could climb out of the fifth-storey window, rappel down to his window, and deliver the gift. Everyone thought it was a grand idea, the only problem being that I would have to get permission from the rector of the seminary to rappel out of his room. Normally one who is in charge of a group of students and could be held liable for their safety isn't going to allow someone to climb out of his fifth-storey window after a party, but we managed to surmount this obstacle by approaching one of the younger faculty members to ask the rector if some students could lower a drink from his window down to the priest on the floor below. This seemed harmless enough, so permission was granted.

We quickly moved into the rector's room, opened the window, removed the screen, and before he knew what was going on, I was outside and rappelling down to the fourth floor. Word of what was about to happen had spread like wildfire throughout the entire student body, which quickly gathered on the lawn below.

Knocking on the window, I finally got the priest's attention. When he opened the window, a roar went up from the student body below. I tapped him on the face and told him to open the screen. I had a gift for him.

When he realized that I was standing on his windowsill, he nearly went into cardiac arrest. Upon recovering from shock, he opened the screen. I handed him the bottle of Scotch, stepped back, and rappelled quickly to the ground.

Most members of that student body no longer remember me, but I'm sure they will never forget the night I delivered that bottle of Scotch to our floor moderator.

This story nearly had a tragic ending. One of my friends was so impressed by the event that he asked me to order a climbing rope for him. Thinking that he would ask me to teach him how to rappel before trying anything, I gave him the rope when it arrived.

Several days later he decided to repeat my stunt and rappel down from the fifth-story window. He tied one end of the rope to the radiator, put on a pair of leather handball gloves, and stepped out the window, intending to slide down the rope. He might as well jumped out the window without a rope. Holding onto a ⅜-inch nylon rope while wearing leather gloves is impossible. He fell to the ground so fast that the gloves burned and the nylon rope melted from the heat of friction. He had rope burns on his hands and a rope burn up one side of his face. Three months later he was still limping as he approached the altar to be ordained.

For some strange reason he never showed any further interest in rappelling.

Seminary life could be rather dull and boring back then, but with a bit of creative ingenuity, some of us managed to make it rather interesting and exciting. The fact that I survived seminary life is to me one of the surest signs that God wanted me to become a priest.

I do have many fond memories of my days in the seminary. Although I didn't realize it at the time, seminary days were carefree days, days free of problems or pressures. At the time I thought studying for a final exam or writing a term paper was rather stressful, but when compared to the problems and difficulties with which a priest is confronted, often on a daily basis, we truly had an easy life in the seminary.

I also have memories of some rather humorous events. At one weekend liturgy, for example, as the priest lowered the chalice after the consecration, he hit the top of the ciborium, and some of the Precious Blood spilled over the corporal. Taking a moment to size up the situation, he called the acolyte over and whispered something to him. The acolyte then lumbered off into the sacristy.

We all knew what conversation had transpired. The priest told the acolyte to go into the sacristy to get some water and a purificator so that he could wipe up the Precious Blood.

The celebrant waited patiently as the acolyte scrambled around in the sacristy. As moments became minutes, we could sense that the celebrant was becoming impatient. Finally, we heard water flowing into a container—it flowed and flowed and flowed. As the water continued to flow, the look of impatience on the celebrant's face gradually turned into one of wonderment. As the sound of flowing water continued, we all knew something big was about to happen, the question was just how big it was going to be.

Finally, the water stopped flowing, and moments later the acolyte appeared, staggering out into the sanctuary with a washtub full of water, enough to wash the altar clothes, the priest's vestments, and the sanctuary carpet. That scene, along with the expression of total disbelief on the celebrant's face, will forever be etched on my mind.

On weekends and on special feast days some of the priest faculty members and seminarians would go to neighboring convents to celebrate the liturgy. On Good Friday one of the priests and several seminarians went to a convent to celebrate the Liturgy of Good Friday. One of the seminarians was an older gentleman, a second career man. When it was time to proceed to the side altar where the Blessed Sacrament was reserved, the priest sent him to the sacristy to get the processional cross.

Apparently the sisters had forgotten to put the processional cross out. In any case, after an unusually long absence, the seminarian came out carrying a large costumer, which stood about five feet high, had a rounded cross bar on top, and rested on two shorter cross legs. Before the priest could stop him and send him back, he started down the center aisle, so the priest followed while the nuns were in stitches.

After the liturgy the seminarian, still unaware of what he had done, was rather indignant with the behavior of the nuns and the way they carried on during such a solemn liturgy. For reasons unknown to the rest of us, he never advanced to Sacred Orders. Some suggested that perhaps he failed to pass the minimum test, namely, that of being able to distinguish a crucifix from a costumer.

In those days, immediately after the reading of the Gospel on the Feast of the Ascension, the Paschal candle was extinguished, symbolizing that Jesus had ascended into heaven. Once, after reading the Gospel on the Feast of the Ascension, the celebrant called the altar server over and said to him, "Extinguish the Easter candle!"

The server gave him a blank look, which only an altar server can give when he has no understanding of what he was told to do, so the priest said to him again, "Extinguish the Easter candle!"

Again, the server responded with a perplexed look. Impatiently, the priest said, "*Extinguish* the Easter candle!"

With that the server walked back to the sacristy and after a few moments came running back with the fire extinguisher.

One is always nervous when doing something new for the first time. For newly ordained deacons, the distribution of the Eucharist for the first time was cause for such nervousness. One poor fellow, who was particularly nervous, placed the sacred host on an elderly woman's tongue, and while raising his hand slightly before removing it, caught her upper plate and pulled her teeth right out of her mouth.

Another classmate, on an extremely hot summer day, tripped on the carpet in the sanctuary in front of a huge fan. As he stumbled to the floor, the sacred hosts spilled from the ciborium and were blown all over the sanctuary. For the next twenty minutes, he and three other priests were crawling around on their hands and knees picking up the hosts.

My weekend assignment during my final year of studies was that of visiting a large children's hospital on Sunday mornings. As I have reflected back upon that experience over the years, I have often thought it would be good if everyone could visit such a hospital once or twice a year. It's difficult to feel sorry for oneself after making such a visit and seeing infants, babies, and small children who are suffering. Some were dying from cancer, and others were paralyzed, or blind, or physically deformed.

How incredibly blessed one is to be born with good health, yet so often we take this precious gift so much for granted.

FATHER JOSEPH A. MIKSCH

JEALOUSY—HOW STUPID CAN ONE BE

S EMINARY RULES AND regulations were rather strict back in the early 1960s. We led a rather cloistered life, almost completely isolated from the rest of the world. While we did have a TV and radio in the recreation room, we weren't allowed to have them in our private rooms. I confess that I did have a small transistor radio, which I kept hidden inside an old book. Nor were we allowed to receive newspapers or secular magazines. I managed to get around the "No newspaper rule" by subscribing to a German newspaper in an effort "to keep up with my German."

We were not permitted to leave the seminary campus unless it was to see a doctor or for some other emergency leave. Once one arrived on campus in early September, the person remained on campus until Thanksgiving break or Christmas vacation.

Although I didn't mind being confined to the campus, I did notice that one of my classmates was gone frequently over weekends and sometimes for three or four days. Since the seminary was too far from home for me to go home for Thanksgiving vacation, I accepted an invitation from a classmate to join his family for Thanksgiving dinner. The next day he took me for a drive around the city. En route we drove past the residence of our classmate who was gone so frequently. His home was a huge mansion with beautiful lawns and bushes spreading out over an entire city block. His folks obviously belonged to the upper class of society.

I was struggling financially at the time. The money I earned from my summer job was enough to get me through the year, and I didn't want to be a burden to my parents, who were already sacrificing much to pay my tuition and help me with other expenses. Consequently, I would work into the wee hours of the morning typing term papers for classmates for ten cents a page. They had to write the papers, of course, but I would type them.

When typing such papers, I always warned friends that I would type the paper as written. I wouldn't be held responsible for misspellings or poor grammatical sentence construction.

One poor fellow wrote a long paper on the Peasants' Revolt, which took place in England in 1381. Unfortunately, he misspelled "peasant" as "pheasant." Toward the end of the paper he made the comment: "This revolt was for the birds." After underlining with red ink every time he misspelled the word "peasant," when the professor came to this comment, he wrote boldly: "This paper certainly is for the birds!"

Returning to the seminary after Christmas vacation, my "rich" friend drove up in a brand new Buick, fully equipped with every possible option. It was his Christmas gift from his parents.

I was driving a beat-up '53 Ford with well over a hundred thousand miles on it, wondering how I would ever be able to afford to buy a better car after ordination, so needless to say, I was a bit jealous.

Several weeks into the second semester of school I noticed our rich classmate was gone on another vacation. When I became aware of his absence, I mouthed off to another classmate in the presence of one of my rich classmate's friend: "I guess if you have money, you can get away any time you wish."

At that my rich classmate's friend became unglued: "Miksch, you stupid dummy!" he said. "Perhaps you're just too stupid and self-centered to notice, but Paul is nearly blind. He's a diabetic! He's already lost sight in one eye, now he's losing it in the other. The reason he is gone so much is because he's going to Boston to see a specialist to see if there's anything that can be done to save what little sight he has in his good eye!"

Wow! I was absolutely stunned! I had no clue that he was bearing such a heavy cross. He was always so upbeat, never complained. I remember going to chapel, where I spent several hours in prayer and in tears, preparing to receive the sacrament of reconciliations. How foolish and small I had been! I was jealous and envious of someone who had a few material things while I had a gift which no amount of money could buy: I had my sight!

I have never forgotten the lesson I learned that day! I am also happy to tell you that in the forty-three years since then I have never been jealous of anyone. There have been many times when others seemed to have it better than I, but whenever I'm tempted to become jealous, I remember that I may not be seeing the total picture. Perhaps the person who seems to have it made has problems or crosses to bear of which I am not aware, or perhaps while they are enjoying good fortune now, their crosses may be awaiting them in the future.

FATHER JOSEPH A. MIKSCH

As I look back on life, I realize how blessed I have been. I often think of my classmate, who spent the final years of his priesthood totally blind, and I thank God for the tremendous lessons he taught me.

He taught me first of all to carry my little crosses without complaining. Although he had already lost sight in one eye and was losing his sight in the other, he never complained. He bore his cross so well, in fact, that I was unaware of the fact that he was carrying it.

Second, he taught me to appreciate my gift of sight. Hardly a day goes by that I don't thank God for the wonderful gift of sight. No matter how foggy and dreary the weather may be, no matter how bleak and barren the winter landscape may be, I look around at the world and find myself praying: "Thanks, God, for this beautiful world! Thank you that I can see!"

When people come to receive the sacrament of reconciliation and confess the sin of jealousy, I give them a few simple words of advice: "Next time you are jealous of someone, just remember that you may not be seeing the whole picture! Perhaps the person you envy has crosses or problems of which you are not even aware. Maybe their crosses still await them in the future. Just take a moment to think about this and take a moment to reflect upon all the blessing you have received—your good health, the fact that you can see, hear, and walk—and give thanks to God for these!"

AN ATTITUDE OF GRATITUDE

D URING THE COURSE of the first ten years of my priesthood I seldom gave much thought to the words of the Preface when celebrating Mass. The Preface was just part of the Mass, the beginning of the Eucharistic Prayer. In an effort to keep from getting into a routine, however, I would use a different Preface each day, one of which read in part as follows:

> You have no need of our praise, yet our desire to thank You is itself your gift. Our prayer of thanksgiving adds nothing to your greatness, but makes us grow in your grace through Jesus Christ our Lord.

Although I prayed these words often, I didn't reflect upon their meaning. This began to change one February day in 1973. I had just taught my last class for the day and was walking back to the rectory early in the afternoon. It was a beautiful day, the first springlike day of the winter. A few, fluffy scattered cumulus clouds were drifting lazily overhead, the temperature was in the upper forties, and the snow was melting, trickling down the gutters, and flowing into the street drains. It was a gorgeous day, a perfect day for flying!

Although I love to fly, I seldom do so during the winter months. It's just too much of a hassle. There are usually snowdrifts around the hangar through which one has to shovel. In order to avoid excessive wear on the engine, one has to preheat it with a space heater before starting it. Furthermore, the Nebraska landscape isn't very beautiful in winter. If snow lay on the ground, everything is white; if there is no snow, the countryside is nothing but a drab brown or gray. Consequently, it had been nearly three months since I was last up in the air. But on this particularly beautiful February day, I felt the urge to go flying.

Driving down to the airport, I shoveled the snow away from the hangar door, spent about an hour giving the plane a thorough preflight inspection, climbed aboard, and took off. Soon I was looking down on the scattered clouds, which hung about three thousand feet above the ground.

Since I was alone, I didn't have to worry about passengers getting sick. Nothing takes the joy out of flying more than having a person sitting next to you, barfing into a barf bag (It spoils the fun for them too!). Thus, whenever I take people up for a ride, I try to keep the plane in straight and level flight, which, quite frankly, can be rather boring!

On this occasion I could do whatever I wanted. Soon I was putting the plane through every maneuver I knew: rolls, accelerated stalls, spins. What a thrill! At times the earth and clouds below seemed to be spinning about. Sometimes it seemed as if the ground were above me or hanging off to the side as I completed steep banks and rolls. What an incredible sense of freedom one has when piloting a plane!

Suddenly, I realized how fortunate I am to be a pilot. Of all the people living in the world only a fraction of 1 percent know the joy I was experiencing. I also realized how lucky I was to have a plane available to me and to be able to fly as often as I do. And so I began to pray: "Hey! Thanks, God, that I can fly!"

My prayer was as simple as that! I recall praying it very loudly so that God could hear me above the roar of the engine.

After spending another half hour in the air, I landed and put the plane in the hangar. Several days later winter returned with a blizzard and heavy snowfall. I didn't go flying again until late in April, but something happened to me that day, and my life has never been quite the same. Now, whenever I go flying, I realize how lucky I am to be a pilot, and I find myself thanking God that I can fly. Because I have become so conscious and aware of this, I enjoy flying so much the more!

Not only have I become aware of my good fortune to be able to fly, but also I have come to realize so many other blessings that I had taken for granted. I can walk! My sister, who had polio when only thirteen, has been confined to a wheelchair for the past sixty-five years. How wonderful it is to be able to get out of a chair and walk about! "Thanks, God, that I can walk!"

I can see! True, I must wear glasses! The last time I renewed my driver's license, when I was taking the eye test, the officer who was conducting the test said, "Fr. Joe, why don't you try it without your glasses!"

I always wear my glasses, but I thought I would give it a try. Pressing my forehead against the eye machine, I squinted as I tried to make sense out of those fuzzy "letters." Slowly I began to read: "E (pause) H . . . D . . . J."

Then the officer said, "They are all numbers, Fr. Joe!"

I must wear glasses when I drive, but I can see! Often I find myself thanking God that I can see. After a period of cloudy weather, when the sun comes out and the sky is so blue, I find myself praying: "Thanks, God, for sunshine and that beautiful blue sky!"

One Easter Sunday, as I was driving down a country road to take Communion to an elderly, housebound parishioner, I spotted a half-grown German shepherd trotting down the road about a quarter of a mile ahead of me. When the dog heard the car coming, it crouched down behind a small clump of grass to hide. When I drove by, it sprang up and barked furiously at me. Looking in the rearview mirror, I could see the "smile" on its face, and I am sure it was thinking, "I really scared that priest!"

It was so comical to see that big dog trying to hide behind that small clump of grass. I had spotted the dog long before it saw me, and I knew exactly what it would do. As I drove on, I found myself praying: "Thanks, God, for that crazy dog!" Then to Jesus, present with me in the Blessed Sacrament, I prayed: "Jesus, Your Father is so good to us! He has created such a wonderful and beautiful world for us. I thank You and Him for that crazy dog!"

Because of that simple prayer, the memory of that Easter morning experience will be etched in my mind forever.

Perhaps a hundred times a day I find myself praying, thanking God for something. My prayers are so simple: "Thanks, God, for . . . !" With each such prayer I have become more aware of God's many blessings, and as a result I have come to enjoy and appreciate life all the more!

Of course, it is easy for me to be grateful to God for His many blessings, because I have been truly blessed. I've had to face very few hardships in life unlike some people who must live with chronic illnesses and pain, or like others who have had nothing but tragedy, disasters, and setbacks in life.

Several years ago, however, I did face a crisis in my life. I had a herniated disk in my back, which caused excruciating pain. Often when I would walk across the parking lot to offer the morning Mass, I prayed to God, asking Him to help me get through that Mass. Every step was painful, and standing at the altar for twenty minutes was almost more than I could endure.

I spoke with several doctors and with others who had back problems. Some had undergone successful surgery, and others continued to live in pain. An awful reality was presented to me—I might have to live with pain for the rest of my life. But even then I found reason to be grateful to God and found myself praying: "Thank you, Lord, for sixty years of life without pain! I took such a precious gift so much for granted! Thank you! Give me the strength to accept Your will whatever it may be!"

I had back surgery on a Monday. The following Sunday I conducted an all-day Confirmation retreat for sixty-six eighth graders. The surgery was so successful!

Now I find myself thanking God often each day for the simple fact that I can stand without pain. I also have much more compassion and understanding when dealing with parishioners who are not so fortunate and must live with chronic pain.

Because of these experiences, I have finally come to realize the meaning of the words of the Preface that God doesn't need our prayers of thanksgiving! They add nothing to His greatness, but I have come to realize how much I need such prayers. My very desire to thank Him is truly a gift!

Now when I introduce the prayer of the Preface at Mass with the words: "Let us give thanks to the Lord our God!" to which the people respond: "It is right and just to do so!" I just want to shout at the top of my voice: "You're darn right! We should *always* and *everywhere* give thanks to the Lord our God!"

When one becomes aware of all the blessings God has given us, especially His greatest blessing, His Son Jesus, and He in turn shed His blood on the cross for us, our only attitude should be one of joyful thanksgiving! So let us give thanks to the Lord our God!

LESSONS IN HUMILITY

HAVING COMPLETED FOUR years of theology after graduating from college, as a newly ordained priest I thought I had finally arrived. Almost the entire parish community in which I grew up joined me for the celebration of my First Mass. Their greetings, words of congratulation, and support, did much to bolster my self-image. I was ready and eager to begin my new way of life as a parish priest.

My bubble burst the day I knocked at the door of the rectory of the parish to which I had been assigned as an assistant pastor. The elderly pastor, who answered the door, greeted me with: "Oh, come in, Sonny boy! I've been waiting for you to arrive!" For the next three years I had to live with that awful title!

The first few months in a rectory for a newly ordained priest can be a very humbling experience. The phone rings, and you answer: "St. Rose Rectory, Father Miksch speaking."

The person asks for the pastor, and you reply: "He's not in."

"May I speak with the secretary?"

"She's out on her lunch break!"

"Is the housekeeper there?"

"No! It's her day off! May I help you?"

"No, thank you, Father. I'll call back when someone is there who knows what is going on!"

If only I would have appreciated those times when people didn't want to talk to be because they knew I didn't know what was going on. Later I would be delighted when a phone call was for the pastor, secretary, or housekeeper, but initially it was a very humbling experience.

My first pastor, an elderly gentleman, spoke and acted as if he knew Abraham and Moses personally. I soon learned, as did so many other newly ordained priests back then, that there was only one way of doing things and that was the pastor's way!

We had curfews in those days. Assistant pastors were expected to be in no later than 11:00 p.m. Often they were not allowed to have keys to the rectory, so if they arrived after curfew, they might not be able to get inside.

One young assistant arrived back at the rectory after curfew and found himself locked outside. Not wanting to wake the elderly pastor for obvious reasons, he surveyed the situation, and then remembered that there was an air duct leading from the roof down into the kitchen. Thinking that he might be able to climb in through that air duct, he climbed up on the roof and descended through the duct, dropping down into the kitchen. It took awhile for him to make his way through the duct. When he dropped down into the kitchen, he was greeted by the pastor and two policemen who were waiting to arrest the intruder.

Sometimes priests, who had been ordained a few years earlier, would play tricks on the newly ordained. They would call late at night, asking the new assistant to come quickly to anoint someone who was dying. Eager to perform his priestly duty, the priest would rush out on his mission only to discover that the address he was given took him to the middle of a cemetery. Fortunately today such shenanigans are no longer pulled.

My first pastor was a rather cantankerous old man with a strong dislike for people in authority. He wasn't exactly a fan of the local archbishop and had no love for anyone who bore the title of monsignor, perhaps because he was never so honored.

On one occasion he was planning to make a trip to Europe, spending some time in Rome. When the archbishop heard that he was intending to go to Rome, he wrote to Father and offered to get him a ticket for a papal audience.

His response was, "No, thank you! I don't need your help to see the pope."

One of the monsignors, who had studied in Rome as a young priest, offered to get him a ticket. Again, the offer was refused. No help was needed from the archbishop or a monsignor; he was quite capable of taking care of himself.

When he arrived at the airport in Rome, a bit confused and unsure as to how to go about getting a ride into the city, apparently his look of bewilderment caught the eye of a man who was elegantly dressed in a business suit. "Can I help you, Father?" he asked.

Father showed the man his hotel reservations and inquired as to how he might get there. The gentleman offered to give him a ride into the city.

Collecting his luggage, the gentleman accompanied the Father out to a limousine parked outside the front door. As they rode into the city, the gentleman introduced himself as the papal ambassador from Sweden. He explained to the Father that he had some business at the Vatican and asked if it would be okay if he took care of that business first, and then he would take the Father to his hotel. Of course, this was agreeable with the Father.

When they arrived at the Vatican, the driver drove through the huge gates and parked in the papal courtyard. While the ambassador and his driver went off to take care of business, the Father remained seated in the car. A few minutes later Pope John XXIII stepped outside and began to stroll through the courtyard. Seeing the Father in the car, he came over, spoke with him, and gave him his blessing.

When the Father returned from his trip, he made it known to the archbishop and monsignor that he didn't go to see the pope. No! The pope came to see him!

Being a very articulate and outspoken man, on another trip to England this priest was with a tour group going through one of the great tourist attractions in England. The guide was going on and on, speaking about the great King Henry VIII. Finally, the Father had enough. At the top of his voice, loud enough for everyone in the group to hear, he asked, "Why don't you tell them the truth! He murdered three of his wives and died of syphilis?"

While visiting in Ireland, he was walking down the sidewalk when he met three Irish bishops. Stepping off the sidewalk, he tipped his hat and bowed reverently as he greeted the bishops, saying: "Good morning, gentlemen!"

They ignored him completely and walked past. "Oh, excuse me!" he shouted after them. "I thought I saw three gentlemen, but I see I was mistaken!"

FATHER JOSEPH A. MIKSCH

YOU WOULD BE SAFER WITH A GOOD PILOT

M Y FIRST PASTOR was a good man, a man of deep faith and firm convictions. He had a generous heart and did wonderful things for many people, but he insisted on doing things his way! He also had some strange ideas, one of which has turned out to be a wonderful blessing for me.

Shortly after I arrived on the scene, he made it very clear to me that he didn't want me associating with other priests for fear that if I did, I might become an alcoholic or a gambler. (As you can see, he regarded his brother priests very highly!)

Over the years he had a number of assistants, most of whom were with him for only a year or two; some lasted only a few months. The one assistant with whom he got along very well happened to be a pilot. Thus, one night at the dinner table, he told me once again that he didn't want me hanging around with other priests, but suggested that I do something constructive like taking flying lessons. He told me he would even offer to help pay for such training.

I had never given any thought to becoming a pilot. I presumed that one had to have perfect vision. Since I wore glasses already when in the fourth grade, becoming a pilot never seemed to be an option for me.

Realizing that I needed some kind of diversion in order to maintain my sanity in this very confining environment, I accepted his offer and soon enrolled in ground school. Eighteen months later I was the proud holder of a private pilot's certificate.

Today, whenever I go flying, I find myself saying a prayer of thanksgiving for this saintly, cantankerous, old man! Being able to fly has added such an incredible dimension to my life!

Flying can be a rather expensive hobby. Small 4-place aircraft rent from between $70 and $100 per hour. I've never had difficulty finding willing passengers to fly with me and share the cost. On a number of occasions I have flown out to Jackson Hole, Wyoming, or up to Glacier Park in Northwestern Montana with three widows, the youngest of whom was eighty. For some strange reason people think that if you fly with a priest, you are safer than if you fly with an ordinary pilot. I tell them they would be much safer with a "good" pilot.

Taking people on such trips has often been good for their prayer life. I once took off on such a trip with three elderly women. Shortly after takeoff I realized that the door was ajar. In this particular aircraft it was impossible to slam the door shut once you were airborne. Rather than circle back for a landing, I decided to fly a few miles on to the next airport, where we landed, closed the door, and took off again. Once the ladies realized the door was ajar, their conversation ceased, and three rosaries were quickly pulled from their purses.

On another occasion we were flying over Rocky Mountain National Park, circling Longs Peak. An avid rock climber, I wanted to get a good view of the east face of Longs Peak; some of the routes up the Diamond are listed as classic climbs in North America. Usually the wind blows up the western slopes of the Rockies and downward on the eastern slopes. I was aware of this and knew that we would be caught in the downdrafts on the leeward side of the mountain, so as we flew around toward the eastern side of the mountain, I made sure the plane was pointed away from the face so that we could fly away from it. I hadn't warned the ladies, however.

As we flew around the east side of the mountain, we suddenly got caught in a three-thousand-foot-per-minute downdraft with the mountain wall shooting upward to our left. At no time were we in any danger, though the ladies didn't know this. One could easily have lost an eye from the rosary beads, which came flying out of three purses.

There is a saying among pilots that flying consists of hours of boredom interspersed with moments of terror and panic. I've had my share of both! After the initial thrill of flying wears off, it does become rather boring just to take off and cruise around. On long cross-country trips one becomes just as anxious to reach one's destination as does one when driving in a car. Thus, the hours in the air can become rather boring.

Then comes those moments of terror and panic! I flew out to Newcastle, Wyoming, some years ago, intending to spend a day or two touring the Black Hills and Devils Tower by air and by car. As I flew over Mondell Field just northwest of Newcastle, I noticed two large white Xs on the main runway, indicating that the runway was closed to air traffic. I had forgotten to check the notams (notices to airmen on current runway conditions throughout the country, which are available to pilots at flight service stations). Had I checked the notams before departing on the trip, I would have known that the airport at Newcastle was closed. As it was, I was low on fuel and didn't want to risk flying another fifty miles to Sturgis, South Dakota. There was a small temporary airstrip on which I could land, but I knew that at this higher altitude and warm summer temperatures I would never be able to get off the ground from such a short strip. I had no choice but to land, thinking that I could ferry my passengers to Sturgis by car, and then take off down the highway next morning if necessary.

Setting down on the short runway, I taxied up to the maintenance building. There I visited with the airport manager. The main runway at Mondell Field is 5,300 feet in length. Right near the middle of the runway a large section of concrete, perhaps 120 feet in length, had been chiseled out, leaving a hole about two feet deep. A ways to the north of the hole stood a stack of crates off to one side of the runway. The airport manager told me that there was 2,600 feet of runway available from the end of the runway to the hole, then 1,500 feet available beyond the hole. He thought that one could taxi down the runway, skirt around the crates and hole, and then use the remaining 1,500 feet of runway to lift off.

That was all I needed to know. If he thought it could be done, I knew I could do it! We spent the rest of the afternoon sightseeing around the Devils Tower, and then spent an enjoyable evening in Newcastle.

Next morning I took on a full load of fuel, taxied down to the end of the runway, and took off. With a fully loaded aircraft, at a higher ground elevation and scarcely any headwind, the plane lumbered along picking up speed very slowly. As we were approaching the crates and the hole in the center of the runway, I realized that we didn't have liftoff speed. I also realized that we were going too fast to swerve around the crates and the hole and too fast to stop before hitting the hole. At the last minute I instinctively pulled back on the yoke, hoping the plane would fly. It did, but just barely! It lifted about ten feet off the ground and mushed over the hole before settling back down on the runway, but now I had another 1,500 feet of runway to accelerate to liftoff speed.

Once we attained rotation speed, I pulled back on the yoke and climbed out over several bulldozers and other pieces of heavy construction equipment. The workmen on those machines were all waving and probably thinking that

I was either the greatest stunt pilot in the world or the craziest fool they had ever seen take off. If they were thinking the latter, they were correct!

I'm sure my three passengers weren't aware of the danger I had just subjected them to so foolishly. I certainly learned a valuable lesson that day and have never flown anywhere since without first checking the notams. I also have a "moment of sheer terror and panic" story to relate!

Flying has also done wonders for my mother's prayer life. Whenever I would tell her that I was planning on going on a trip, she would immediately begin praying and would pray almost constantly until I returned safely. On several occasions, when flying through thunderstorms, I am convinced that it was her prayers that got me through. Once when flying through miserable weather, I was wondering how I would ever get back to the plane's home base where weather conditions were well below minimum requirements. As I approached the airport, however, suddenly the ceiling seemed to lift and visibility increased dramatically. I landed safely, but before we could climb out of the plane, fog again enshrouded the airport. Thanks, Mom!

The greatest joy I have experienced as a pilot has been when I have an opportunity to take some elderly person up for their first plane ride. My oldest passenger to date was a woman who was ninety-four. She scarcely slept the week before the ride; so anxious and nervous was she, but after that first ride, she is ready and eager to go any time.

Taking students up for a plane ride can be a wonderful way of establishing a special relationship with them. I also use the offer of a plane ride as a carrot to encourage them to be faithful to their serving assignments as altar servers. Each time a boy or girl serves, he or she is graded on a 1-10 point basis. Every now and then, the three with the highest point totals get to go up for a plane ride.

In one high school where I taught, I decided to teach an elective course in Aviation Science. The course was anything but easy, but some of the boys, who liked to mess around and didn't care to study, signed up for it. I realized almost immediately that it was going to be a long year unless I took control of the class immediately. Thus, as soon as the school year began, I took each of these boys up for a plane ride alone and made sure he used the barf bag. Upon landing, I would say: "Gee, you really are a pansy! Tell you what, I won't tell anyone about this if you promise to shape up in my class!"

It was mean! It was cruel! I've confessed it when receiving the sacrament of reconciliation, but it also worked! We had a very successful aviation science class that year, no disciplinary problems, and I am happy to report that one of those students now owns his own plane and another eventually joined the air force and learned to fly.

FATHER JOSEPH A. MIKSCH

MIRACLES OF GRACE

REFLECTING BACK ON forty-three years of priesthood, I realize how blessed I have been and am happy to be where I am in life. I have experienced many joys and successes in my ministry, but I have had difficult times too, times of failure, disappointment, and loneliness. While I certainly have enjoyed the good times, I would never want to eliminate the difficult times, for at such times I was most aware of the power and the presence of God in my life.

Above all, I treasure most those times in which I was privileged to witness miracles of God's grace at work in the lives of others.

I remember one such time when I had just finished proclaiming the Gospel on Easter Sunday and was about to begin my homily when a man entered and stood in the back of the church. His grubby cutoff jeans and dirty sweatshirt suggested that he was not a regular churchgoer.

It was terribly distracting to see him standing there, and I really had to concentrate as I preached my homily. Already I knew what to expect after Mass. He would be camping at my doorstep, give me a long sob story, and ask for a handout. Just what I didn't need on this particular Easter Sunday!

Sure enough, after Mass, there he stood in front of the rectory. "Father," he asked, "can I talk to you for a few minutes?"

I tried to be polite as I invited him inside, but my thoughts weren't so kind. Veteran panhandlers know when it's best to ask for a handout. They strike at the most inconvenient time, knowing that you will give them something just to get rid of them.

He looked at me for a moment, and then began to stammer. "I really don't quite understand why I'm here," he said. "When I left Omaha this morning for (he mentioned the name of some small town in South Dakota, which I can no longer remember) . . ., I didn't even realize it was Easter. But, somewhere along the way, I took a wrong turn and ended up here."

"You know, it's so strange," he said, "as I was approaching the outskirts of the town, I became so curious. I decided to drive up and down the streets just to see what this town was like. When I drove past your church and saw all those cars parked outside, I just felt such a strong urge to go inside to see what was going on. I walked in right as you were beginning your sermon."

"I know!" I thought to myself." You created such a distraction I forgot half of what I wanted to say!"

But the stranger kept on with his story, and I remained silent. "I haven't been to church for ten or fifteen years," he said. "As I listened to your sermon, you said something that really touched me. I wonder, would it be possible for me to get back in the church? Could I go to confession?"

I still was not convinced he was sincere; I thought it might be part of a clever pitch for a handout. I questioned him about a few things, to see if there were any reasons why he couldn't receive the sacraments. There were none, so I helped him make an examination of conscience, after which he made a thorough confession.

Then I invited him back into church to receive the Eucharist, sharing with him Luke's account of the appearance of Jesus to the disciples on the road to Emmaus; I related it to his experience of the Risen Lord on his way to South Dakota.

Afterward, as he was getting into his car, he paused. "Ah!" I thought, "now he will make his pitch."

"Father," he said, "I apologize for taking so much of your time. Please accept this as a token of my appreciation." He pulled $20 from his wallet and gave it to me.

As I drove home that afternoon, reflecting on our visit, I tried to figure out what I might have said in my homily, which I had blown because of him, that so touched him. The more I thought about it, the more I came to realize that it was nothing I had said. I simply had been given the privilege of being the lucky individual to witness a miracle of God's grace.

Then there was the time when I received a call from a nurse at the local hospital asking me to visit an elderly gentleman who was asking for me. The ninety-two-year-old gentleman was a complete stranger to me, but his wife knew my mother. Thus, over the years they had kept track of my whereabouts and activities through articles and news items, which appeared in the local newspapers. She was a devout Catholic; he belonged to no church and had never been baptized.

During the course of that first visit, I concluded that it was more her wish that I come to see him and not his. We had a pleasant visit, however, and he responded positively when I offered to pray with him.

I made it a point to visit him on a regular basis three or four times each week. I noticed that he seemed to be troubled when we said the Lord's prayer; he had a difficult time with the words "Forgive us our trespasses as we forgive those who trespass against us."

Our visits were always pleasant. I think Carl looked forward to them, and I was beginning to enjoy our newly formed friendship. We would visit about the weather, reminisce about the past, and then conclude with prayer and reflection on some scripture passage. One day, after about a month of such visits, his wife followed me out of his room and said to me, "Father Joe, I think Carl is ready for baptism if you would just ask him."

I went home and prayed about it, carefully considering how I would approach the subject. While Carl was always friendly and eager to pray with me, I sensed that his wife was rather pushy about his becoming Catholic, and he resented that, thus I didn't want to make the same mistake. At daily Mass I asked the school children to pray with me for a very special intention. Several days later when I went to visit Carl again, we talked about all sorts of things. I was delighted that his wife was not present, thinking that I could approach the subject better alone, but just as I was about to ask Carl if he had ever considered being baptized and becoming a Catholic, his wife walked in. "Carl," she said, "don't you think it would be a good idea if Father Joe baptized you?"

Carl turned away from her and me in obvious anger. "Now don't start that again!" he growled.

"Woman! You really blew it this time!" I thought to myself. At that moment I thought we had lost the opportunity to persuade Carl to accept baptism. Seeing that he was angry, I tried to calm him.

"Carl," I said, "it would obviously make your wife very happy if you were baptized, but the only way I could ever baptize you would be if it were your own decision. It would be wrong for you to be baptized just to please your wife or me."

I continued to visit Carl on a regular basis and prayed with him. About a week later, one of his nurses called again and asked me to bring some literature explaining the Catholic faith. Carl had asked her to request this of me.

When I went to visit Carl the next day, he told me he had been thinking about what I had said and was interested in becoming a Catholic. I gave him a crash course in Catholicism, explaining only the basics of our faith, realizing that his time on earth was running out. After a few instructions Carl was baptized, confirmed, and received his First Communion. For the first time, when we said the Lord's prayer, I sensed that Carl was very much at peace.

After the ceremony Carl looked up and said to me, "Father Joe, you have done more for me than all the doctors and nurses have ever done."

A few days later I anointed Carl and gave him the Eucharist for the last time. An hour or so later he slipped into a coma and died a very peaceful death. Again, I realized that I had been privileged to witness another miracle of grace.

On yet another occasion I received a call from a parishioner who had surgery for throat cancer three or four years earlier. In recent weeks she was having trouble swallowing. Her general physician confirmed that the cancer was coming back and had set up an appointment with her specialist.

She called me the day before her appointment with the specialist. I visited her, heard her confession, administered the sacrament of the anointing of the sick, and gave her Holy Communion.

She called me late the next evening when she returned from seeing the specialist, apologizing for calling so late in the evening.

"Father Joe," she began, "I just had to call you and tell you what has happened! When you placed your hands on my head and anointed me yesterday, I felt this tremendous sense of peace. I just felt that I was going to be okay. I went to bed last night and slept soundly throughout the night, something I haven't been able to do for months. This morning when I woke up, I felt so good, I just knew everything was going to be okay."

"When the specialist walked into the examining room, the first thing he said to me was: 'I had this strange feeling this morning that when I would examine you I would find nothing wrong.' He then put the scope down my throat and examined me. He did so for such a long time that I began to worry. I tried to study his face to see if I could see any negative reaction and was really getting worried. Finally, he stepped back, shook his head, and said, 'I can't understand it! There is no sign of cancer! There's nothing wrong with you!'"

"Father Joe! It's a miracle!" she told me.

Whether it was a miracle or not, I don't know. I do believe that God sometimes does choose to exercise His healing power through the sacrament of the anointing of the sick. When that happens through my ministry, I can only step back in fear, wonder, and awe! My reaction on such occasions is much like that of St. Peter as recorded in Luke's Gospel. At the sight of such a huge catch of fish, Peter could only respond to Jesus: "Depart from me, Lord! I am a sinful man" (Luke 5:8).

At such times when I am privileged to witness such miracles of grace and see the saving power of God at work among us, I can only step back in wonder and awe and thank God for choosing me to be a priest!

WHEN WE PUT OUR SIMPLE GIFTS IN THE HANDS OF THE LORD

B ECAUSE WE'VE HEARD the Gospel narrative so many times, often we fail to listen. We no longer ask questions about Jesus and His miracles. We've lost our sense of curiosity. It was only after I had been a priest for some years that I came to realize this. One Saturday morning a young man rang the rectory doorbell. He was very nervous; he was interested in becoming a Catholic.

We visited for about an hour, during which time I explained what our program of instructions was all about. I learned from our discussion that he knew almost nothing about God or Jesus. At the end of our meeting, I gave him a copy of the New Testament and placed a marker at the beginning of the Gospel of Luke. I told him to read the first few chapters of Luke's Gospel and scheduled a meeting for the next weekend to discuss what he had read.

I was in for quite a pleasant surprise when he came back a week later for instructions. Along with the copy of the New Testament, which I had given him, he had a spiral notebook filled with questions. Not only had he read the first few chapters of Luke, he had read all four Gospels and was well into the Acts of the Apostles. It was all so new to him—and so exciting!

He had questions about everything! When he read about the miracle of the multiplication of the loaves, for example, he wanted to know just what took place. Did Jesus multiply the loaves, or did the loaves remain the same size as the disciples broke off pieces and distributed them to the crowds? Obviously, I had no answers to many of his questions, but what an experience his questions turned out to be for both of us. I suddenly came to realize how much I had taken for granted. I began to read the scriptures with a renewed sense of curiosity and in the process gained many new insights.

As I reflected with him upon the miracle of the multiplication of the loaves (John 6), I came to a much greater appreciation of the narrative. Formerly I viewed the account as just one more miracle which Jesus performed in the presence of His disciples. Now, however, I read it in a totally different light. In fact, I am absolutely convinced that this particular miracle can take place over and over again even in our own lives.

The crowd was enormous! When Jesus asked Philip where they could buy bread for so many, he replied, "Not even with two hundred days' wages could we buy loaves enough to give each of them a mouthful" (John 6:7).

Andrew came along and said to Jesus, "There is a boy here who has five barley loaves and a couple of dried fish, but what good is that for so many?" (John 6:9).

Jesus took those few loaves and two fish, blessed them, and told His disciples to distribute them. Not only did everyone have enough to eat, twelve basketsful of pieces were left over after everyone had been satisfied.

Sometimes we look at the many problems in the world around us. There are so many needy people: the hungry, the lonely, the elderly, the homeless. It's easy to throw up one's hands in despair and say, What can I possibly do to solve all of these problems?

But Jesus doesn't ask us to solve all of the problems of the world; He just asks us to do our part. And if we place our simple gifts and talents in His hands, only God knows what miracles can take place!

The life of Mother Teresa is proof of this. She certainly didn't set out to become world famous, nor did she ever dream that she would touch so many lives. She simply placed her simple gifts in the hands of the Lord, and He made the miracle happen.

Mother Teresa was once asked by a reporter: "Don't you become discouraged when you see so many suffering people in the world? You do such wonderful work, but you can't possibly help all of them."

With a smile she replied, "Oh, I know that I could never help all the needy people in the world. I just try to love them one at a time."

Because she placed her simple talents into the hands of the Lord, Mother Teresa touched countless thousands. Many of her religious brothers and sisters are now working in the slums among the poorest of the poor in many countries throughout the world. Again, the miracle of the multiplication of the loaves has taken place through the life of this saintly woman.

I firmly believe that similar miracles can take place in our own lives if we put our simple talents in the hands of the Lord. With how many people does each of us come into contact during the course of our lives? With how many people do we rub shoulders each day at home, at work, in the community? How many people will you as parents touch through your children and grandchildren?

I like the story told about Pope John XXIII. Shortly after he became pope, he visited one of the parochial schools in Rome. He asked the children, who were so excited and overjoyed to see him, who they thought was the most influential person in the world. Every hand went up; they all answered that it was him.

He smiled, shook his head, and then mentioned a woman by the name of Marianna Roncalli. The children looked puzzled; they didn't recognize her name. John XXIII then explained that she was his mother. He said it was she who prayed for him when he was a small boy that he would become a priest. It was her prayers and good example that inspired him to do so. Had he not become a priest, he would never have become a bishop, a cardinal, or the pope. "So," he said, "she is the most influential person in the world."

As I reflect back upon my years of priestly ministry, I wonder how many people I may have touched for the better in some way. I wonder how many people may have been influenced by my homilies, or by my writings, and through conversations with me. Only God knows!

Sometimes a mere word of praise or a compliment can make all the difference in another person's life. One day after teaching school in our parish high school, I stopped to make a visit in church. A seventh-grade girl was playing the organ, with her music teacher sitting nearby. I waited until she finished, and then complimented her and asked if she would consider playing the organ at one of our children's liturgies. She beamed with pride as she looked at her teacher, who nodded approvingly. Some weeks later she played at Mass, and I again complimented her. A few weeks later I was transferred to another parish and forgot about this brief encounter.

Twenty years later someone sent me a clipping from the school newspaper. Apparently alumni were encouraged to write about teachers who had made a difference in their lives. This lady had written about my words of praise and encouragement and how they had led her to choosing music as her major in college and serving as a parish liturgist and music teacher. I felt flattered, but soon forgot about the compliment she had paid me.

Ten more years flew by. Our parish placed an ad in a number of national music publications stating that we were looking for a parish minister of music. This lady, now married with a family of four, sent me an e-mail, once again thanking me for having played a major role in her choice of careers. She stated that she was presently serving as parish liturgist and minister of music in a large city parish and had taken her choir to Italy, where they sang in Assisi and Rome. She also stated that whenever a child exhibited some musical talent, she remembered how I had encouraged her and so she tried to do the same.

Recently, I received a call from this woman's sister, who called to inform me that her sister had lost her battle with cancer and had just passed away. She told me her family wanted me to be informed because I had been such a great influence on her life.

What a lesson this has been for me! What a difference a word of praise can make in another person's life! With fear and trembling, I also wonder how many people I may have influenced in a negative way through some thoughtless comment, sarcasm, or bad example. I can only pray to God, ask for His forgiveness, and pray for those whom I may have offended or affected in a negative way.

I suspect most of us will be overwhelmed and surprised at the end of our lives when we stand before the judgment seat of Almighty God and come to realize how we have touched and influenced the lives of so many people around us. No matter how insignificant we may think our gifts are, if we place them in the hands of Jesus, the miracle of the multiplication can take place all over again!

THE PRIEST TOOK THEM ON THEIR HONEYMOON

G REG AND JANET had known each other for nine years before they began to date. They were good friends, but their differences in faith kept them from dating or considering the possibility of marriage. Janet was a strong Catholic, who served as parish liturgist for a number of years. Greg was a theology student, studying to become a Lutheran pastor.

Ironically, while it was their faith that kept them apart, it was their faith that also brought them together. Because they were both so strongly committed to their faith traditions, they were constantly challenging each other's beliefs and questioning the reasons for those beliefs. An intense, but respectful, rivalry developed between them. In the process both grew stronger in their individual faiths and in their respect for one another. Through this process they gradually came to realize that they were no longer just friends, but that they truly loved one another and wanted to spend the rest of their lives together as husband and wife.

Janet had been in my junior religion class some twelve years earlier, and I had recently been reassigned as pastor to her home parish, so she introduced Greg to me. We all were a bit nervous and apprehensive during our first visit, but it didn't take long before we felt at ease in one another's presence. Before long we found ourselves engaged in conversations that could last for hours. We could joke, laugh, share personal experiences, and discuss the various doctrinal differences between our two faiths.

At times these discussions became rather intense, and even emotionally charged, but we always parted respecting one another for our commitment to our beliefs. Greg went through our RCIA program in order to learn more about the Catholic faith, while Janet went through a similar program conducted by the local Lutheran pastor. They made a Christians Encounter Christ weekend and went to Engaged Encounter. In addition, we spent long hours many an evening discussing our two faith traditions. No couple I have ever worked with spent so much time in preparation for their marriage. Through it all we became very good friends.

Six weeks before the wedding, as one of our long sessions was coming to a conclusion, I asked Greg and Janet if they had made any honeymoon plans.

They hadn't, so in jest I suggested that I could rent a small plane and fly them out to Grand Teton National Park and serve as their mountain guide. We all laughed at the thought, and they parted.

Three weeks later, Janet called. "Father Joe," she said, "you weren't serious when you suggested that you take us on our honeymoon, were you?"

No! I wasn't! But it was obvious that after giving it some thought, they were. And so it came about! Three weeks later on a Saturday afternoon I officiated at their wedding. The following Monday I met them at the airport to take them on "our" honeymoon.

Having never been on a honeymoon before, I had no idea how much luggage a young bride and groom could take along. The Cessna 182 RG was loaded to capacity and probably over gross weight.

We flew over the Wind River Range en route to Jackson Hole. Once there, Greg and Janet split, spending three days touring the area alone while I camped out at the Climbers Ranch and did some hiking and rock climbing. We then got back together to spend a day hiking up Cascade Canyon before flying back home over the Absaroka and Big Horn Mountain ranges.

Now I am one of the few priests in the country who can talk about what he did while on a honeymoon!

IN CHRISTIAN MARRIAGE YOU BECOME
THE SACRAMENT

DURING THE COURSE of the past forty-three years I've had the privilege of officiating at more than four hundred marriages. Each wedding is unique and special because each couple is unique, but there is one wedding that truly stands out in my mind as being special.

As I was working with this particular couple in preparation for their marriage, I learned that the parents of the groom were both totally deaf. I also learned that many of their hearing-impaired friends would also be attending the wedding. Thus, we made arrangements to have a minister present who ministered to the deaf, to interpret the liturgy in sign.

Never having had the opportunity to work with the deaf, I vividly remember the occasion. Before the ceremony, as I was putting things in order in the sanctuary, I noticed that when people who were deaf entered the church through a side door near the front of the church, they would pause and look out over the congregation. If they spotted their friends and acquaintances, they would immediately carry on a conversation in sign. I watched with amazement as they communicated so effortlessly with one another from a distance.

Throughout the ceremony the minister stood in the sanctuary in a prominent place and interpreted the prayers, readings from scripture, and the exchange of vows in sign.

After the exchange of rings, a meditation hymn followed. The guitarist was a professional, and the vocalist was equally talented; the music was beautiful. I sat in my chair with my eyes closed as I drank in this magnificent sound.

About half way through the song I opened my eyes and looked about. The minister stood in the sanctuary, translating the words of the song into sign language while indicating with a rhythmic gesture that it was music. It was then that I realized how awful it would be not to be able to hear! I suddenly realized that no one could describe music to a person who has never heard sound. Music is something one must experience. Nor could one describe color to a person who was blind from birth; color is something we must experience for ourselves.

As I reflected back upon this experience, I came to realize that love is much the same. If a person has never experienced a deep, loving relationship with another human being, and unfortunately there are many such persons who were abused and battered as children, such a person would have a difficult time understanding us when we try to describe what love is all about. Love is something we must experience before we can fully appreciate it.

Likewise, a person who has never experienced a deep human love relationship would have a difficult time understanding what we are talking about when we talk about God's love for us.

Jesus was aware of this. When He taught us to pray to God as "Our Father in heaven," He knew that if we have had loving parents we could get some inkling of an idea of what God's love for us is. The more deeply we experience human love, the more we can come to appreciate and understand God's love for us.

In speaking of the love that exists between a husband and wife in Christian marriage, St. Paul says, "This is a great mystery; I mean that it refers to Christ and His Church" (Eph. 5:22). In other words St. Paul is saying that the love that a husband has for his wife and she for him is a reflection of the love that Jesus has for His Church. This is how Christian marriage becomes sacramental.

What's so beautiful about Christian marriage is that the husband and wife are being called by God to reflect His love to one another. They become living signs, "sacraments," of His love to one another!

Jesus loves us unconditionally. He loves us when we are good, but He also loves us when we sin. Even after they had nailed Him to the cross, He prayed: "Father, forgive them for they know not what they do" (Luke 23:34).

Husbands and wives are called to love one another unconditionally too. They promise to accept each other as husband and wife "in good times and in bad, in sickness and in health, until death." In the many ways in which they live out these vows throughout their wedded life, they reflect to one another the love that Jesus has for all of us. In the many ways in which they show their love for one another, by caring and showing concern for one another, by their willingness to forgive, by their acceptance of one another, they are reflecting to one another the acceptance, the care and concern, and the forgiveness that Jesus extends to us. Through such experiences of human love, couples can grow in their understanding of the love that Jesus has for His people, His Church.

Husbands and wives not only share their sacrament with each other, they also become sacraments to their children. Children who are brought up in a home environment that is filled with love can begin to appreciate and understand at an early age what it means to call God a "loving Father."

Couples also share their sacrament with the community in which they live. I think of one woman, for example, whose husband was suffering from Lou Gehrig's disease. She had invited me over to share a meal with them one evening. Her husband could scarcely talk anymore; it was extremely difficult to understand what he was trying to say. But he knew well the prognosis of his illness. Eventually his throat would become so paralyzed that he would have to be fed through a tube in his stomach. As he told me what lay ahead, he expressed the fear that he would have to go to a nursing home and worried about who would take care of him. At this point his wife gently placed her hand on his shoulder and said, "You'll stay right here, Gene. I'll take care of you."

Tears still come to my eyes as I recall that beautiful gesture and expression of love. That woman did take care of him to the very end and, in doing so, set a beautiful example for all the members of her community of just how deep human love can be. Through her beautiful example of loving care, we all came to a better understanding of the depth of human love and to a greater appreciation of what God's love is all about.

The wedding season has already begun. Again this year, like so many other priests and ministers throughout the country, I will be officiating at a wedding nearly every weekend from mid-April until November. Frequently, in my homilies on such occasions, I tell couples about that "special wedding" at which I was privileged to officiate as I try to impress upon them the sacredness of their vocation, for as married persons they are being called by God Himself to become "sacraments" of His love to one another, to the children God may grant them, and to the entire community in which they live.

I invite their families and friends who are present to join me in asking God to bless them with a love that is truly sacramental, a love that is reflective of the love that Jesus has for His Church, and I assure them that if they strive to reflect His love to one another, their marriage will be successful no matter what the future may bring.

I also love the account of the wedding at Cana recorded in John's Gospel (2:1-11). Jesus and His disciples were invited. Perhaps because they were, they ran out of wine. It was Mary who first noticed it. She called it to the attention of Jesus, who then worked His first miracle and changed water into wine—a lot of water into wine! Six stone water jars holding from twenty to thirty gallons, that's a lot of hooch! Perhaps this is why I like the story so much! I love a good party.

The fact that Jesus provided such a plentiful amount suggests to me that Jesus wants us to enjoy life, not just in eternity, but also here on earth.

But what I really like about this account is the fact that Jesus was invited! I often wonder: Was His name at the top of the list of guests to be invited? Was He a good friend of the bride or groom, or of one of their parents? Or was He perhaps an afterthought? Perhaps someone suggested that He be invited since He was beginning to make a name for Himself. We don't know the circumstances or reasons why He was invited. The important thing is that He was invited!

Because He was invited, the wedding at Cana has become the most famous wedding that has ever taken place! Today, nearly two thousand years later, we still talk about it. On some weekends throughout the year this wedding is talked about in every Catholic church throughout the world.

I often share this Gospel narrative with engaged couples or mention it in my wedding homilies. No one will be talking about their wedding two thousand years from now in Asia, Africa, or other parts of the world, but I do believe that if they do invite Jesus to be a part of their marriage, and make sure that He is always an invited guest in their relationship and in their home, two thousand years from now they will be celebrating their love for each other in His presence in heaven.

NEVER CHARGE A MOOSE!

E VERY NOW AND then when I walk into a classroom in our elementary grade school, one of the students will plead: "Father Joe, tell us another bear story!"

Encounters with bear while spending my summers working in Grand Teton National Park have given me quite a repertoire of stories that fascinate children and help break the monotony of normal class presentations.

My dad had a great love and appreciation for the outdoors and the beauty of nature. As I have already mentioned earlier, he shared this love with me through such simple statements as "Isn't that a beautiful full moon! God is so good to give us such a beautiful world in which to live!"

Because of his great love for the outdoors, and especially for the mountains, I too have become enthralled with the beauty of nature. One summer evening in 1959, Dad was reading about the national park system and how many college students were employed during the summer months to work in the parks and surrounding tourist areas. I knew immediately that this was for me!

Throughout the winter months of 1960 I wrote to every national park in the country, inquiring about jobs. I shared my enthusiasm with several of my college classmates, one of whom was an army veteran. I soon learned that such jobs were difficult to get unless one had friends in Congress or other high places in government. Veterans were given first chance at such jobs, so my veteran friend landed a job in Grand Teton National Park.

The following summer I rode out to the Tetons with him as he was returning to his summer job with the Park Service. Thanks to him for putting in a good word for me with his boss, I managed to land a job with the Department of the Interior, working on trails in Grand Teton National Park. I held that job for the next four summers, working roughly from Memorial Day till Labor Day.

For a young man with an adventuresome spirit, who loved the outdoors, one could hardly consider such employment a job; it was more like being on a paid vacation throughout the summer months.

At that time there were about thirty young men employed to maintain the roughly three hundred miles of hiking trails which led through the canyons and up the mountain slopes of Grand Teton National Park.

Throughout the month of June we worked on the lower trails, or shoveled snow on some of the high mountain trails. I remember cutting steps through the snow over one of the high mountain passes on August 1, 1962.

Usually four men worked on a crew. Often a crew would be assigned to work in a certain canyon for the entire summer, maintaining perhaps twenty miles of trail. Around July 1 we would backpack into a canyon, set up a cook tent and sleeping tent anywhere from five to eight miles from the nearest parking lot, and then work in the backcountry from Monday through Friday.

Every day was a new adventure. Some days were spent hiking the trails, carrying a cruiser ax and a two-man crosscut saw. Our job was to clear the trail of any timber that had fallen recently. On some such days we found few downed timber and spent the day enjoying the hike. On other days we might come across a huge tree that covered many feet of the trail. We might spend three or four days working hard to clear such trees.

While I tend to idealize those wonderful, carefree days of my youth, the job wasn't always fun. Often we had to work in the rain. The trails would be muddy and slippery, and the grass and abundant foliage alongside the trail would soon soak our boots and clothes. Often the temperature in the high country would dip below freezing during the night. I remember some mornings crawling out of my sleeping bag to find that my wet pants had frozen and stood out stiffly when I picked them up. It was no joy slipping into such frozen pants!

Charging a Moose!

On one occasion a college friend of mine was passing through Jackson Hole. I agreed to meet him for a night out on the town. At the time I was working in the backcountry from Monday through Friday. My foreman told me I could hike out to see my friend, but I had to be back in camp by 8:00 a.m. next morning for work.

I had to hike about six miles from the parking lot to base camp, so I started up around 6:00 a.m. About three miles up the trail I came to a stretch where a vertical rock wall rose above one side of the trail and dropped vertically into a canyon on the other side. Fifty yards ahead, coming up the trail was a large bull moose.

There was no way whereby I could get around the moose. I couldn't climb above the trail—the wall was too vertical, nor could I climb down on the other side of the trail. Somehow I had to get past the critter in order to get back to base camp.

Pausing for a few moments, I finally thought I might be able to scare the critter. I took off my jacket and hard hat, and started swinging them in the air as I ran toward the moose, yelling and screaming. When I had covered half the distance separating us, I realized the bluff wasn't working. The huge beast had put his head down and was pawing the trail with his front feet as he was getting ready to charge. With that I threw my hard hat at it, then my jacket, turned around, and started running back up the trail with the moose in hot pursuit. Coming to some huge rocks bulging out of the rock wall, I found several good handholds and managed to climb about fifteen feet above the trail. There I hung on for dear life with the moose snorting and stomping around on the trail below. For what seemed like an eternity the huge beast stomped about just a few feet below me while I prayed with all the fervor of my heart: "Pray for us sinners *now* at the hour of my death!"

Finally, the beast tired of this game and sauntered slowly up the trail, stopping every now and then to look back and stare at me. When it was finally far enough up the trail, I climbed down, ran down the trail to retrieve my jacket and hard hat, and raced down the trail, arriving breathlessly at the base camp in time for work, with a story of adventure, which I can tell for the rest of my life.

During the summers that I worked in the park and later while spending many vacations in the park, I've developed a great respect for moose. They can be more dangerous to humans than bear are. They hang out in marshy and willowed areas, thus one often stumbled upon them at close range. What can be most frightening is to stumble upon a calf, not knowing where the cow is. One certainly does not want to venture between a cow and its calf!

Back in the early 1960s when I worked in the park, we drank water from the streams and lakes and never got sick. I lost my appetite for such stream water, however, one time when we hiked up Paintbrush Canyon and found a dead moose lying in the stream from which we had been drinking.

Reporting our find at park headquarters, our crew was given one of the nastier jobs I had while working in the park. Since it is almost impossible to dig a hole in such rocky ground, our foreman sent us back into the canyon with about twenty gallons of crankcase oil to burn the moose carcass. Well, let me tell you, burning a moose is no picnic! Moose don't burn very well! After two days of futile effort at this grizzly job, we persuaded the foreman to let us take several pack horses back into the canyon with which we pulled the carcass out of the stream and into the forest about fifty yards below the trail.

Encounters with Bears!

Black bear are rather numerous in Grand Teton National Park. Generally, they are harmless and prefer to stay away from humans. It's only when they lose their fear of humans and discover that humans are a food supply that they become a threat. As the saying goes: "A fed bear is a dead bear!" Once a bear loses its fear of humans, then it has to be transported deep into the forest away from human contact.

During the summers that I worked in the park, I always kept a wary eye out for bears and remained a safe distance away whenever I encountered one. Running from a bear is what one's natural instinct tells you to do, but it's the wrong thing to do. If you run, the bear thinks you are prey. Since a full-grown bear can run faster than a race horse, it can run down even the fastest human in a matter of seconds. With claws three to four inches long, black bear can run up a tree almost as fast as they can run on the ground. Thus, one learns to observe them from a respectable distance.

Living in the backcountry for five or ten days at a stretch, we often encountered bears. One summer a two-year-old decided to spend some time hanging around our camp, much to our dislike. Had it gotten into our food supply, we would have been some very hungry campers. Although we pelted it with rocks in an effort to drive it away, it continued to remain close to our camp.

One morning it climbed high up in a tree next to the trail. A wrangler came by, leading a string of perhaps twenty tourists on horseback. We knew that if they spotted the bear, there would be tourists around our campsite all day long. We had to go to work and were fearful that if people hung around our camp all day, some things might be missing. Thus, we didn't say a word about the bear.

Neither the wrangler nor the tourists noticed the bear, but their horses did. They were snorting and nervously jumping about as they passed beneath the bear tree. The wrangler was busily shouting out, trying to calm them. We watched in silence as they all passed and then hiked off to work.

Having the bear around our camp was not to our liking. One night after I had gone to bed I heard the critter sniffing around just outside our tent. Suddenly it poked its nose through the flap. Since the tent didn't have a back entrance, I did the only thing I could do; I grabbed a stool and whacked the bear over the head as hard as I could. It let out a loud yelp and took off, much to my relief!

One morning I looked out of my tent and saw the bear nearby. It was standing in such a way that just its rump was visible. The wind was blowing from the bear toward me. I thought to myself that if I sneak up on it, I could break its back with a sledgehammer and then kill it. No longer would we have to worry about our food supply.

Grabbing the sledgehammer, I began to tiptoe toward the bear. As I began to raise the sledge for a swing at the bear, I tripped over a tree root. With that the bear took off, and I survived to tell the story.

As I reflect back upon that experience today, I realize how foolish I was. Had I injured that bear, I would have been in big trouble. As fast as bears are and with their long claws, I wouldn't have had a chance.

On another occasion one of my trail mates and I came upon a large patch of delicious blueberries. We stopped to enjoy a meal. As I foraged through the patch, devouring the succulent juicy-sweet berries, I would talk occasionally to my partner. At first, he would respond, but after a while he no longer did, so I finally looked up to see where he was. Much to my surprise, he was nowhere to be seen, but less than twenty feet from me was a bear in my blueberry patch. Slowly, very slowly, I backed away and moved down the trail.

One of the fellows with whom I worked was nearly deaf. He wore two hearing aids, and even then could hardly hear. When his batteries wore out, he couldn't hear us at all.

Once when we came back to base camp, we chased a small bear cub up a tree. Dave, the hearing-impaired man, decided to try to rope the cub. What he planned to do after that, I don't know. In any case, he climbed up a larger tree near the bear cub and was leaning out toward the cub, trying to slip a rope around its neck.

While he was doing this, mother bear came along. She did not take kindly to the idea. Fortunately for Dave, the tree on which he had climbed was too fragile to support the mother bear's bulk, so she climbed up another tree next to the one in which Dave was. Meanwhile we were standing below, yelling to Dave, trying to warn him of the danger he was in. Not being able to hear, he thought we were cheering him on, so he kept leaning out toward the cub while mamma bear was reaching out with her front paw, trying to knock him out of the tree, missing him by only a foot. Finally, Dave looked around and saw mamma bear almost on top of him. He nearly fell out of the tree and ducked into a nearby shelter for cover. Meanwhile mamma bear and her cub climbed down the tree and took off into the forest, much to everyone's relief!

One of the nice things about meeting tourists in national parks is that they all have a common interest and love for the outdoors. Thus, they are usually friendly and ready to strike up a conversation with anyone. Since we were working on the trails, most tourists presumed that we were park experts. And so we became such!

Oftentimes people wanted to know the names of some of the surrounding peaks. We were quick to tell them: That's "Miksch's Butte" or "Miksch's Peak." Some would take pictures and jot down the name in a notebook. What a grand feeling to have a mountain named after you!

A lot of people had concerns about poisonous snakes. Fortunately there are no poisonous snakes in the Tetons, but when people would ask us, we would tell them about the "snow snake," the only really deadly snake in the park. A white snake with pink eyes, they are usually found near snow; they are very fast and have a deadly bite.

After telling people about such stories, we would watch as they approached a nearby snow bank. Sometimes they would venture off the trail and bushwhack through dense brush in order to stay clear of snow and these deadly vipers.

At other times we would carry on conversations that would confuse tourists. For example, we might be walking down from Lake Solitude when we would meet a group of people hiking up toward the lake. We would greet them, and then one of us would comment to the other: "I wonder how far it is yet to Lake Solitude."

The people we had just met would all pause, look around bewildered, and then get out their maps, studying to see where Lake Solitude was. Such were the capers of the trail crew workers of my day.

Yes! I have confessed all these shenanigans.

TRANSFIGURATION IN GRAND TETON
NATIONAL PARK

I T WAS IN the Tetons that I came to a deeper appreciation of the Gospel account of the transfiguration of Jesus on the mountain.

In the book of Wisdom (13:5) we read the following text: "From the beauty of the created world comes a corresponding perception of the greatness of God the Creator." Often during my days in the Tetons I felt the presence of God in the beauty of the mountains. One experience I will never forget is one that I described in an article entitled "Transfiguration in the Grand Teton," which was published in the Catholic Digest, August 1990.

It had been raining, drizzling, and foggy for nearly two continuous weeks, and everyone's patience had worn to a frazzle.

"We've driven two thousand miles to get here to see the mountains," one disgruntled tourist said, "and the only mountains we've seen have been on postcards."

At the time, I was working for the Department of the Interior in Grand Teton National Park, and, along with about thirty others, maintained the three hundred miles of foot trails in the park. We'd clear fallen trees, shovel snow at the higher elevations, and build rock drains and simple log bridges. Occasionally, we constructed new sections of trail.

Since we worked outside all day, the rainy weather was hard on us too. The trails were slippery and muddy. It was impossible to keep our clothing and boots dry.

One night the wind really kicked up, and our crew leader was concerned that timber might have gone down in some parts of the forest, blocking the trails and making it difficult for horseback riders to get through. So next morning when we reported for work at park headquarters, he sent us off in pairs to check the various trails.

Another worker and I were assigned to check out the Glacier Trail. On any other occasion I would have been delighted. Beginning at the Lupine Meadows at an elevation of 6,740 feet, the trail leads upward almost five miles to Amphitheater Lake. Because of the grand views one has of Jackson Hole from the upper sections of this trail (9,698 feet), it remains one of my favorite trails in the park.

But it wasn't on this occasion. The trail was muddy and slippery. I knew that, for every step forward, we would slide backward two or three inches. The hike, we could tell from the start, would take us all day. And it would be cold and nasty.

Grabbing a crosscut saw, a cruiser ax, and a backpack into which we had packed a first-aid kit, extra clothes, and our lunches, we had set out. Soon our feet and legs were wet from sloshing through puddles of water and trudging through the wet underbrush. We only had to clear a few small trees from the trail.

After hiking several miles and gaining about eight hundred feet in altitude, we entered the base of the clouds and walked into dense fog. We couldn't see more than one hundred feet in any direction. It was gloomy and chilly. Hiking under such miserable conditions made the distance between each switchback on the mountain seem endless. Had this been a clear day, the beauty of the mountains, meadows, flowers, trees, and the valley stretching out below—all would have held our attention, but not on this day.

We hiked several miles under dismal conditions and gained a lot of altitude before we realized that our surroundings were gradually brightening. Suddenly, we saw something we hadn't seen in nearly two weeks: a small patch of blue sky. As we climbed higher, we realized we were emerging above the cloud layer; the sun began to break out from behind the clouds.

We arrived at Amphitheater Lake around 11:30 a.m. Leaving our saw and ax on a rock, we continued to climb still higher up the steep eastern slope of Disappointment Peak until we were completely above the clouds. The view below is one I will never forget. The entire valley was filled with billowing white clouds, dazzling in the sunlight. Some twenty miles across the valley, peaks from the Gros Ventre and Absaroka ranges rose above the clouds. Behind and around us the mighty granite peaks of the Teton Range towered above, reaching into the bright blue sky. Neither of us had a camera, but the scene will never be erased from my mind's eye.

As I stood there, gazing in awe at the beauty around us, I suddenly experienced for a brief moment an awesome and overwhelming sense of the presence of God. While it is impossible to describe such an experience, it truly has made an indelible impression upon me. Like Peter, who wanted to erect three tents and remain there forever, one wishes such a feeling could last forever, but just that quickly the experience ended.

We shed our wet boots and socks and basked in warm sunshine for three hours. I've never enjoyed the sun more; it felt so good to be warm!

All too soon it was time to head back down to meet the truck that would pick us up and take us back to park headquarters. As we descended back into the clouds, we quickly became cold and wet again.

The three or four days that followed continued to be damp and dreary, but my experience on the mountaintop—the blue sky, the incredible view, the warmth of the sun—helped me hang on and look forward to the day when the inclement weather would dissipate and all would be bright, dry, and warm again.

Every year, when the feast of the Transfiguration comes around and I read the Gospel narrative in which Jesus took Peter, James, and John up on Mount Tabor and there revealed His glory, I reflect upon my experience above the clouds. Just as those couple of hours in the warmth of the bright sunlight gave me a more positive attitude throughout the wet and dreary days that followed, the times when I have felt the touch of God have helped me through those times when He does not seem to be present.

Such moments usually come suddenly and unexpectedly. I may step outside and witness a beautiful sunset or gaze up at a starlit sky. Suddenly, I am overwhelmed with a sense of God's presence.

The first time I stood on the rim of the Grand Canyon and gazed at the beautiful and immense abyss, which dropped away before me, I felt God's presence. And I've experienced His presence in the quiet of a church as well as during the celebration of the Eucharist. I've visited with parents who have had similar experiences of God's presence as they witnessed the birth of their children.

Such moments happen only rarely in my life, but what overwhelming experiences they are! Like Peter, I can only exclaim: "Lord, how good it is for me to be here!"

Great spiritual writers like St. John of the Cross and St. Teresa of Avila speak of such moments too. They point out that these moments when God seems to break through and touch us with His divine presence are gifts, grace. They tell us that there is nothing we can do to bring about such experiences. We can pray for days, weeks, and months—and God still may seem so distant. Then, suddenly God is there! All one can do is enjoy these experiences and be grateful to God for them.

Just as Jesus's glory was revealed to Peter, James, and John to strengthen them for the difficult days to come, I believe that God gives us these special moments of "transfiguration" to help us through the difficult times in our lives. God gives us these moments to strengthen us so we might be faithful as we journey through life.

When we wonder about God's existence, such revelations will sustain us. In them, we are given a promise and a glimpse of the Creator's glory, which we will enjoy for all eternity in His kingdom in heaven.

FATHER JOSEPH A. MIKSCH

OBEDIENCE—A BLESSING

AFTER BEING IN school continuously for twenty years, I had enough of school. Throughout the summer months after my ordination I was looking forward to the beginning of the school term in September. I fully intended to drive around town past local high schools and colleges on the opening day of the school term, just to watch students going to class and rejoicing over the fact that I was free and out of school!

A week before that blessed day was to arrive, I received a letter from the archbishop. The line that caught my attention read as follows: "You will be teaching at Paul VI High School this fall!"

Bishops and archbishops have such a direct way of putting things! Others might have written it like this: "Have you ever considered teaching in high school?" or "Would you like to teach?" or "Would you like to think about teaching in high school?" No! The message was direct and clear: "You will be teaching at Paul VI High School this fall!"

I spent the next twenty-five years teaching on a part-time basis in Catholic high schools, and I am so glad that I did. I discovered a talent I never knew I had, and I certainly learned to think on my feet. I also discovered that so much of what I taught in the classroom I could also use in adult education classes and in my homilies.

Although I was afraid when I first walked into the classroom because the students seemed to be "so cool," self-confident, and disinterested, I soon discovered that high school students are still little children—just their bodies are bigger. Once one sees beyond that "cool" facade, one discovers beautiful people who are full of life, energetic, optimistic about the future, eager to learn, filled with enthusiasm for life, and hungering for God.

When the day finally came when other pastoral responsibilities required that I give up teaching in high school, I realized just how much I enjoyed being with young people in the classroom and regret very much the fact that I no longer have that opportunity.

Through it all, I've also learned a valuable lesson about obedience. Had my bishop given me a choice, I would never have chosen to enter a high school classroom and would never have discovered the talent I have as a teacher.

And so it has been with other priestly assignments! I have come to realize that if I were given a choice, I would probably choose assignments that were very safe and similar to what I had already done. In so doing, I would feel safe and secure. But by being assigned to very different assignments, I have been forced to grow and stretch and thus continue to discover talents I never knew I had.

At one point a few years after I was ordained, I was pressured by another priest into conducting a retreat for which I felt I was totally unqualified and unprepared. I survived the weekend, but came away feeling like a miserable failure. My self-esteem was at an all-time low.

After reflecting upon that experience for a few days, I decided I would never again be pressured into doing something I really did not want to do. I had a brilliant idea! I came up with four excuses, which I could use to get out of doing something when someone called. I typed these up and left them by my phone. The excuses were something like this:

"Gee, I would love to do that! When will it be?" Once I was given a date, I would pause for a few moments, and then reply: "I'm sorry! I already am booked that weekend! Perhaps I could help you next time!"

I'm ashamed to confess that for three or four years I used these excuses until one day the Holy Spirit caught up with me and awakened me. Someone had called and asked if I would be willing to help with a project. I declined, using one of my excuses. After I hung up, I began to feel guilty. Suddenly I found myself thinking: "Joe, you big dummy! If you keep this up, your brain is soon going to shrivel up, and you won't have anything to offer to anyone!"

As I thought about this and prayed about it, I made a commitment to myself that I would say yes to doing two new things a year. They could be work-related things or fun things, but each year I would say yes to doing two things I had never done before. This idea was not original with me. Father John Powell suggested it in one of his books, and for this I will forever be grateful!

I made that commitment to myself twenty-five years ago, and it is one of the best things I have ever done for myself. I have grown so much in the process. Today when the phone rings and I'm asked to do something new, I still ask the question: "When will this be?" I then check my calendar, and if I am free, I say yes!

In the process I have learned that I have many more talents than I realized. Most often I do succeed and do a reasonably good job. When I do, I receive positive compliments and come away feeling good about my accomplishments. Furthermore, next time I am asked to do something similar, I am no longer afraid because I have already done it successfully.

I have also learned that there is a benefit when one fails. On those occasions when I have bombed out, those people no longer ask me to help them, and I have a little more time to relax. I no longer feel so bad when I fail as long as I feel that I have done my best under the circumstances.

My world has expanded so much since I made that decision to do new things each year. Being a rather shy fellow by nature, when I would go on vacations, I usually went as a "tag along" with others who would make most of the arrangements, but as I gained more confidence in myself, I began to step out on my own and discovered an entirely new world of excitement.

I've been an avid rock climber for years, an interest that doesn't appeal to most of my flatlander friends in Nebraska. One of my goals was to go to Switzerland to climb the Matterhorn. Realizing that I would never be able to persuade any of my friends to join me on such an adventure, I finally decided to go alone. Twice I have flown to Switzerland, taking nothing but a backpack, tent, and sleeping bag, and spent two wonderful sixteen-day vacations climbing in the Alps. In the process I discovered the joys of traveling alone. I could go wherever I wanted to go, I could sleep in the forests, and I could get up at 4:00 a.m. and take off on a long mountain hike. I didn't have to worry about what others wanted to do.

Today when I am preparing couples for marriage, I encourage them to make a commitment as a couple to doing two new things a year in order to help keep their relationship exciting and alive. By so doing, they can look forward with anticipation to that new activity; they will have a shared experience together upon which they can reflect back later in life, and in the process they may discover a whole new world out there that they never knew existed.

PARENTS—REFLECTIONS OF GOD'S LOVE

S OME YEARS AGO a young couple invited me over to their home for Sunday dinner. It was a beautiful summer day in early July. When I arrived at their home, the wife met me at the door and informed me that her husband and son were in the backyard by the swimming pool. She ushered me through the house to the back door where her husband greeted me and invited me to join him by the pool.

While we sat together on a bench, their little four-year-old son, Christopher, whom they called "Topher," climbed up onto the high diving board, looked at his dad with a big smile, and said, "Watch me, Daddy!" With that he dove into the pool, came up sputtering and spitting when he surfaced, then swam to the side of the pool, and ran around to climb up onto the diving board again.

As we sat there and watched the little guy expend some of his boundless energy, his dad told me how it all began earlier that morning. He was swimming in the pool when Topher climbed up on the diving board. Although he had been up there a number of times before, he had never had the courage to jump. On this particular morning, however, he walked out to the end of the board and was looking down at his dad. He was afraid, but his dad kept reassuring him that it was all right and kept coaxing him to jump: "You won't get hurt! You'll be okay! Daddy is here to look out for you!"

Finally, after a long while, the little guy got up enough courage to jump. He hit the water hard, swallowed half the pool, but came to the surface coughing, spitting up water, and laughing all at the same time. He swam to the side of the pool, climbed the ladder, and was ready to jump again. He hadn't stopped since.

I don't know whom I enjoyed watching more that day, little Topher jumping off the diving board, or his father who was beaming with such obvious pride and joy in his son's accomplishment.

So often I find myself listening to parents as they tell me about their children, their faces aglow and beaming with pride. I think of one young mother telling me about her son who was in fifth grade and thinking about becoming a priest. He had his own altar in the basement, and even a confessional made from a cardboard appliance box. He "celebrates Mass" on a regular basis for the children in the neighborhood.

His mother told me that her Protestant neighbor's little girl was in such a hurry to leave the house one Saturday morning. When her father asked her where she was going, she breathlessly exclaimed: "Andy is having Mass in five minutes!"

I think of the delight on another mother's face as she told me about her son. He went outside one morning and was sitting beside his dog on the front steps of the porch, where she overheard him say, "Jake, today I'm going to teach you all about Jesus."

I've seen such joy and pride written all over the faces of parents with tears glistening in their eyes as they watch a son or daughter walk up to receive a high school or college diploma, a scholarship, or a certificate of recognition on honors night.

I remember talking to a "soccer mom." During the course of our conversation she said to me, "Father Joe, there may be twenty-two kids out there on the field, but I watch only one!"

Recently, all these memories flooded through my mind as we prayed the Responsorial Psalm at Mass. The response was taken from Psalm 149.4: "The Lord takes delight in His people."

What a comforting thought! Yes! Why wouldn't the Lord take delight in us in much the same way that parents delight in their children?

As we prayed that response, I thought of a passage from the book of Job in which God says to Satan, "Have you noticed my servant Job, and that there is no one on earth like him, blameless and upright, fearing God and avoiding sin?" (Job 1:8)

I also reflected upon the Gospel account of the baptism of Jesus in Jordan by John. The voice of the Father is heard to proclaim: "This is my beloved Son. My favor rests on Him" (Matt. 3:17).

Yes! The Lord does take delight in His Son, and in all of His sons and daughters. I find this thought to be so very warm and comforting. Now when I am privileged to witness the love parents have for their children and listen as they tell me about their accomplishments with obvious pride and delight, I think of this Psalm. In much the same way, only infinitely more so, the Lord takes delights in us, His people!

I also listen as parents share their worries and concerns for their children. I can't imagine what a parent goes through the first time a teenage son or daughter drives away in the family car. They want to go with them, they wish they could be driving for them, but they know they have to let go and let them venture out on their own, but all the while that their children are gone, they are constantly thinking of them, worrying about them, and praying that they return home safely.

Just as parents love their children and want only good things for them, so God loves us with an infinite love and wants only good things for us. But because He has given us free will, He respects our freedom and allows us to make choices. We can choose to draw near to Him, or we can turn away from Him.

The thought of God waiting anxiously for us to return home to Him at the end of our lives, like a parent anxiously awaiting a child's return late at night, is also very comforting!

FATHER JOSEPH A. MIKSCH

THE FAMILY OF THE YEAR

I WAS ONCE asked to sit on a committee of the Knights of Columbus to select a family to be the recipient of the "Family of the Year" Award. Here are some factors to be considered when choosing the family of the year:

1. Has the family made significant contributions to the church, community, and/or council?
2. Does the family enjoy one another?
3. Does the family share experiences?
4. Does the family pray and attend Mass together?
5. Does the family spend time together interacting instead of watching TV?

We had a number of special families who would have been worthy recipients of the award, and it was difficult to select just one, but finally a decision was made. The family chosen was indeed very active in the church. Both husband and wife were leaders in the youth ministry program and willing workers at the annual parish bazaar and dinner. Dad was active in the Knights of Columbus and a faithful volunteer whenever parish projects came along. Mom served as parish organist and director of the youth choir; she was also a member of the parish council and liturgy committee, and taught CCD.

Although it was often difficult for this family to attend Mass together since Mom played the organ at several weekend liturgies, she would often return with her family for a third weekend liturgy. Frequently, she and her two-year-old daughter would attend daily Mass on those days when she didn't have to drive fifty miles to attend her college classes.

Were these parents doing a good job of sharing their faith with their children? That question was answered when the mother overheard her four-year-old son talking to the family dog one morning as he was sitting on the front step. "Jake," he said, "today I am going to tell you all about Jesus." Then he proceeded to share his faith and knowledge of Jesus with the dog.

It was this gesture that won the family the prestigious Family of the Year Award. Not only were the children being evangelized, but also the family dog!

The award was to be presented to the couple at the annual awards banquet, a lavish affair to which many KC dignitaries had been invited. Numerous awards were to be presented, but the climactic moment was to be the presentation of the Family of the Year Award.

Unfortunately, the couple selected to receive the Family of the Year Award was not present at the banquet. When this was brought to the attention of the Grand Knight during the banquet, he sent his wife scurrying off to the telephone. Half an hour later midway through the speeches and presentation of various awards, the couple arrived, entering hand in hand, all smiles, ready to receive their award.

It was only after the banquet when I went up to congratulate them that I learned the real truth about the family of the year. The reason why they were so late was simply because they had forgotten all about the awards banquet. It had been one of those horrible days when everything went wrong. Working hard all day trying to catch up on a week's work, they growled and snarled at one another and the children whenever their paths crossed.

When the wife of the Grand Knight called to see if they were coming to receive their award, both were still in their grubby clothes. Mom was busy scrubbing down her greenly-painted four-year-old son. Although he was not Irish, he had decided to color his entire body green with a magic marker in honor of St. Patrick. By her own admission his mother stated that she was scrubbing a little harder than was really necessary, thank God without a wire brush.

The two-year-old had just gotten her bath and was prancing about in her birthday suit, dancing about in a pile of freshly washed laundry. Realizing the potential consequences, the mother was yelling to her husband and oldest son to put a diaper on her before she had an accident. They were unconcerned and nonchalantly went their way when soon the foreseen accident happened—all over a hard day's clean laundry. It was then, with the room still resounding with expletives deleted, that the phone call came from the wife of the Grand Knight.

I chuckled as I listened to this account of a day in the life of our newly honored family of the year. I suspect that if one kept track, there were more days like the one just described than days of loving, peaceful family togetherness.

FATHER JOSEPH A. MIKSCH

Reflecting upon this humorous event, I posed this question to myself:

If we had known what their family life was really like, would we have chosen them as the family of the year? The answer came immediately: Of course we would have! It's precisely because there are so many days like this in the life of every family that I believe every family deserves such an award!

I recall the days when I was a student in the seminary. Every now and then one of our professors would give a talk in chapel in which he would speak about all the sacrifices we would have to make as priests. I was naive enough to believe this and really felt that I was making a great sacrifice in becoming a priest. Admittedly I do make sacrifices from time to time. But only after I became a priest and became active in family ministry did I realize who really is making the sacrifices. I watch single parents, or mothers whose husbands may not be Catholic, coming to Mass on Sunday with an infant in one arm, one or two other toddlers clinging to her skirt and a six-year-old tagging along behind in a daze, too young to realize that Mom could use someone to open the door. I see such parents and think to myself: What an awesome responsibility! Four little ones totally dependent upon you every minute of the day! It's rather obvious who is making the sacrifices! It certainly isn't me!

I think of the sacrifices parents are willing to make for their children. I think of one couple, for example, who lived on a farm. They loved the farm and were well established. It was the way of life they both loved. They were surrounded by relatives and friends with whom they had grown up. But one of their children suffered from severe asthma attacks and allergies, so the family sold the farm and moved to a western state.

What an incredible sacrifice to leave the farm and the way of life they loved, to leave family and friends behind, to take up a new career far from home, yet they did so without hesitation. The life of their child was at stake!

I'm grateful to such parents. They are such an inspiration to me and challenge me to become less selfish and more giving to others. I see how busy parents are and know their days and nights are filled with hassles, conflict, and crises as they struggle to raise their children. I think every family deserves to be chosen to receive the Family of the Year Award!

ROCK CLIMBING IN THE TETONS

VISITING WITH PARENTS who have small children often causes me to realize how spoiled I am as a priest and how parents constantly make sacrifices for their children. As priests, we can take a day off each week to get away and relax. Parents with small children seldom, if ever, can take a day off away from their family. As priests, we can plan and take a two-week vacation every year. Most parents spend their vacation a day at a time taking care of sick children.

Over the years I've visited with many dads who never see their paycheck. Their wives open the mail, deposit the check in the bank, make house payments, car payments, payments for the orthodontist—the list goes on and on until there is nothing left. As a priest, my paycheck is mine to spend as I please. I am free to blow it all on myself, give some to charity, help needy families with tuition assistance, electric bills, or whatever. It's mine to do with as I please!

With regard to vacations, I get to determine when, where, and how I will spend it. Again, I don't have to consider where a spouse or the children would like to go on vacation, nor do I have to use my vacation taking care of sick children.

Some people feel that we priests have to make so many sacrifices! Sorry! That's not the way I see it! So often I have been deeply touched by the willingness with which parents sacrifice for one another and for their families.

As for me, when I plan a vacation, I look to the west to the mountains and visits to our national parks. My favorite place is Grand Teton National Park, which I refer to as "my second home." Having spent four summers maintaining the park's three hundred miles of trail, the park contains so many wonderful memories of exciting and adventuresome times. Thus, I make an effort to return to the park at least every other year and spend a week hiking or climbing. What I love so much about such vacations is that they provide me with an opportunity to forget about all the worries and concerns I may have back home. I can leave doorbells and telephone calls behind and enjoy solitude, peace, and quiet. A rock climb in the Tetons requires one's full attention and concentration. Everything else is pushed from one's mind. The beauty and grandeur of the scenery and the excitement and exhilaration of the climb also make one very much aware of the beauty and greatness of God the Creator and draw one into deep communication with Him.

A flatlander from Nebraska who used to be afraid to climb a stepladder, I'm not a great rock climber, but I do enjoy the challenge of a climb and have spent many wonderful vacations climbing in the Grand Teton Range in Wyoming. During the summers in which I was employed by the National Park Service, I climbed most of the Teton peaks, but several eluded me. Thus, it was always my goal to go back and climb those two remaining peaks.

Sometimes in my homilies I point out that Christians can learn much from great athletes. That's not a new idea. St. Paul came up with the idea nearly two thousand years ago when he wrote the following: "Athletes deny themselves all sorts of things. They do this to win a crown of leaves that wither, but we a crown that is imperishable" (1 Cor. 9:25).

Great athletes must become single-minded and remain focused on their goal—the dream of winning an Olympic gold medal or a national championship! They practically give up all else in an effort to attain that goal.

In my quest to climb Mt. Moran and Mt. Owen in the Teton Range, I too had to focus on that goal. In the summer of 1988, I reached my first goal and stood on the summit of Mount Moran.

Two years later I planned to return to the Tetons to climb Mt. Owen. I enlarged a picture of the mountain and had it made into a calendar, which I hung on my bedroom wall. For nearly six months, when I awoke at 5:00 a.m. to jog and get into condition for the climb, I would look at that picture to remind myself why I was getting up so early and spending so many hours in grueling exercises to get into physical condition. The jogging and the long hikes were good for me not only physically but also spiritually. As I focused upon the climbs, I was also reminded of the fact that I need to keep focused upon my ultimate goal in life, namely, to attain the fullness of life with God in heaven.

I started up the mountain around noon on July 11. Six miles later near the timberline, I waited at a designated spot for my climbing partner, Jon Berger, to arrive. Jon was a professional guide, who had climbed extensively in the United States and abroad.

We roped up and then hiked several miles, traversing icy slopes and several glaciers en route to a campsite on a pile of rocks in the middle of the Teton Glacier.

I don't think I slept a wink that night. The rock on which I was lying sloped downward a trifle to my right, just enough to make it uncomfortable and requiring me to brace myself to keep from sliding off. Consequently, I could never relax completely. I had taken three aspirins in an attempt to dull any aches and pains from the long day, but these didn't seem to calm me. I suspect the excitement and anticipation of the climb also had something to do with my inability to fall asleep. I felt comfortable, however, and felt that I was getting some rest.

As the sky darkened, I began to watch for the first stars to appear. Closing my eyes and trying to sleep, I would open them a few minutes later and look again at the stars, the silhouette of the mountains, and the lights down in Jackson Hole. It was a wonderful time for reflection and prayer.

As I lay there, I realized how fortunate I have been to do so many adventuresome things. Had I chosen any other vocation in life, I probably would not have been able to do all the things I have done. I definitely would never have given any thought to becoming a pilot and most likely would never have climbed a mountain.

Once the sky was totally dark, the stars began to shine brilliantly. The Milky Way became so bright that individual stars became visible to the naked eye. I recognized many of my friends: the constellations and stars I knew by name; I began to feel very much at home. The North Star seemed to be a little higher in the sky too, since we were several hundred miles farther north.

I watched the stars, closed my eyes, tried to get comfortable on my tilted rock, would slide a bit, then readjust my position, zip up my sleeping bag, and open my eyes again to gaze at the stars.

Around midnight the moon rose over the Absaroka Range. I watched it rise and gradually climb into the sky. As it did so, it became brighter and lighter outside. The glacier and the snowfields stood out in contrast to the darker ridges, pinnacles, and peaks. It became bright enough that I could recognize all the major features on the mountains around us.

Although I felt as though I had gotten some rest, I never did fall asleep for fear that if I did, I might slide off the rock. I envied my climbing partner, who seemed to be sawing logs throughout the night. Around 2:00 a.m. I woke him. Wolfing down a sandwich and drinking a small can of orange juice, we strapped on our crampons, slung our daypacks over our shoulders, grabbed our ice axes, and set out across the glacier to the base of the climb.

At first we moved along a bit more rapidly than I would have liked, but as we approached the alluvial fan and started up the snow, we slowed down considerably. Each step forward took us six inches higher. Near the top of the snowfield we had to negotiate several crevasses. We gained altitude quickly and soon stepped off the snow onto the base of the rock. Looking down, we had already come quite a distance from the boulder field where we had spent the night.

The description of the route up this first band of rock is rather simple:

> The first section of this couloir, containing rotten rock, is usually capped by a small waterfall from the melting snow on the broad bench about one-third of the way up to the col. Climb up to the waterfall, where a traverse to the left leads to moderate rock on the left wall that takes one to the bench.

From this description I expected the climb up the rock to be a mere scramble. It was for perhaps a hundred feet, but when Jon uncoiled his rope, I knew the scramble had come to an end and the technical climbing was about to begin. Slipping my ice ax into the loop of my daypack, I watched as Jon climbed the first pitch of about eighty feet.

I tried to note each handhold and foothold he used so that I could do the same, but soon he moved around an overhanging rock and out of sight. I was always glad to see the rope go out quickly as it meant the climbing was easy, but when the rope would scarcely move, I knew I was in for a difficult stretch.

Finally, Jon began to pull the remainder of the rope up quickly until it was tight. I yelled: "That's me!" And heard him yell back: "On belay! Climb!"

"Climbing," was my reply as I started up the rock. There were plenty of hand—and footholds and several good jam cracks for lieback holds. Soon I was up the first twenty-foot stretch. Moving around the corner of the overhanging rock, I saw Jon another fifty feet above me. The pitch was more difficult than I expected, but I was able to find enough holds to work my way up.

Once I completed the pitch and was off belay, Jon studied the face, looking for the easiest way up the next pitch. He started up one crack, but soon retreated and tried another. Again I watched as the rope fed out. Every time it would stop or slow down, I would worry about what lay ahead.

Climbing in this fashion for four or five pitches, we gradually worked our way up to the top of the rock band. The climbing was much more severe than I had anticipated. Several pitches were very difficult with few hand—or footholds, but I was securely belayed, so I wasn't afraid. My fear was rather that I wouldn't have the ability to climb a pitch.

A few times when I did look down, I realized that we were already very high above the snowfield from which we had begun the climb. Once up the rock band, we headed up the snowfield that covered the bench and continued up a narrow couloir in which the snow lay at a steeper incline. The climb up the couloir was much longer than it appeared to be when seen from the glacier. As is so often the case when looking up a ridge or face, much of the ridge was concealed from view. It's really impossible to get a true perspective of a ridge until one is on it.

I was getting winded and several times would lean forward over my ice ax and rest for a moment. At such times I would have time to think about where I was, and I could feel myself becoming anxious and a bit panicky, but I would quickly have to regain my composure. Once we would start out again, I had to concentrate totally on what I was doing, and such feelings would vanish.

It is difficult to describe the feeling I had as I looked down over Jackson Hole and saw the lights of park headquarters, and Moose and other settlements. We seemed to be so far removed from the rest of the world, so high above, conscious and alert, while the rest of the world was still asleep. It was a uniquely beautiful experience. So quiet, so peaceful, so far removed from the noise of everyday life. The silhouettes of the mountains around, the whiteness of the snow and granite rock standing out in the moonlight, the freshness of the predawn air—all added to the pensiveness of the moment. We were still a part of this world and yet we seemed to be so far removed

FATHER JOSEPH A. MIKSCH

from the rest of the world around us. We had no contact with those below amid those dots of light, and they were totally unaware of our activity high above. I thought about some of the "out of body" experiences people talk about who have had near-death experiences and wondered whether people didn't have similar feelings at such times. It was an experience like no other I have ever had, one which I truly savored and enjoyed. It is this experience that, I believe, keeps calling me back to the mountains, a deep down longing to be in communion with God.

Onward and upward we climbed. I presumed we would remain on the snow for some time, but after we had climbed perhaps five hundred feet, we traversed off the snow to the left and onto the rock.

The west face of East Prong towered above, in places overhanging. Looking up the vertical face, I knew we still had some distance to go to the col, but we had come a long way.

The predawn light began to brighten the eastern sky as Jon traversed off the snow couloir and onto the rock to our left. Soon he pulled up the slack in the rope. As it became taut, I yelled, "That's me!"

Jon replied, "On belay! Climb!"

"Climbing," I replied, and cautiously left my relatively secure place in the bergschrund, scrambled over talus slopes, and then up a chimney about forty feet to the place from which Jon was belaying me.

For the next four hundred feet we remained on the rock just west of the couloir. At times we could walk a short distance together or scramble up easy rock from ledge to ledge, but at other times we had to climb vertical pitches up chimneys, jam cracks, and rock faces. Several such pitches were extremely difficult. There were times when I really didn't know where to go. Usually at such times Jon could look down from his belay stance and see me; he would give advice as to where he found a handhold or how to make a lieback move. Sometimes there really wasn't much of a hand—or foothold, but if one moved quickly across a friction slab, one could get to the next good hold before gravity would cause you to slip off the rock.

It was enjoyable climbing, each pitch offering a challenge and a feeling of satisfaction when completed. The climbing was also becoming hard work. Often I would bang my helmet against an overhanging rock or find my ice ax or daypack jamming against the rock. My old camera also took a beating. There were times when the last thing I could have cared about was my camera; it was just in the way up some difficult pitches.

Several pitches, which I definitely did not enjoy, were unpleasant because in some of the more critical sections there were mud and grass on the ledges.

Thus, one was unable to get a firm grip on any holds. At such times I really appreciated the belay from above, though I was able to climb all the pitches without having to rely on the rope.

Eventually we could look directly across Glacier Gulch and see that we were even with the summit of Disappointment Peak. At 11,616 feet, we had only another couple of hundred feet to go to reach the col. Already the snowfield on the col seemed to be very near. Traversing a bit to the left (west), we scrambled up the final section of rock.

Slipping our ice axes out of our daypacks, we walked out onto the snowfield on the col. It was everything I had imagined it to be and more! The upper section of the couloir dropped nearly vertically to the south and very steeply to the north, plunging down into Cascade Canyon. To the west of the col the ridge widened out and became a broad snowfield leading up to a 120-foot band of rock up which we had to climb in order to reach the upper snowfields.

There were several routes one could choose to climb this rock band. We paused for a few moments to study the face, and then chose the chimney route. Traversing to the right of the ridge crest along the base of this rock band, we entered the large chimney, the lower section of which was still filled with snow. The rocks were wet and slippery, so we had to climb cautiously.

Taking the lead, I climbed about half way up the chimney, and then belayed Jon up to me. Although icy cold water from snow melting above was trickling down upon us, my nylon jacket and pants kept me relatively dry. By this time my boots were wet, so it didn't matter if I sloshed around in the water.

I had read about climbers climbing up waterfalls, but never quite understood how this was possible. I always thought of waterfalls in terms of a river plunging over a precipice and couldn't imagine how one could climb up such a thing. This particular waterfall was more like climbing up a ladder to the roof with water from a garden hose trickling down over the edge of the roof and down upon the ladder.

Near the top of the chimney we bypassed a clockstone, an overhanging rock, to the right. Although the climb up the chimney was up vertical rock, there was an abundance of good hand—and footholds. My camera took a beating, however, and my backpack with the ice ax jammed against the rock several times.

Once out of the chimney we stood on the ledge about three feet wide at the base of a huge snowfield that was much steeper than I had anticipated. Instead of traversing the snowfield, we were able to walk around it on a narrow ramp, which varied in width from three to ten feet. The snow had melted enough that the rock ledges all around the base of the snowfield were exposed, providing an easy route around it.

Although the exposure to the east and later to the south was terrific, I was too busy concentrating on where I was walking to notice.

The ramp certainly wasn't like a city sidewalk. We scrambled over and around boulders and up ten-foot pitches, but compared to what we had climbed while ascending the couloir, it was a "piece of cake." My only regret is that we didn't take time to enjoy this section of the climb. I also regret the fact that I didn't take time to take more pictures.

The view from the ramp was absolutely incredible and fantastic! We could look directly down upon the Teton Glacier from which the North Face of the Grand rose and towered high above us. Far below we could look out over the glacier moraine, Delta, Amphitheater, Surprise, Taggart, and Bradley lakes, and out over Jackson Hole. Unfortunately, because we were always moving, we didn't take time to enjoy the view.

In several areas along the southern part of the snowfield we made our way over grassy ledges. I felt less secure on the grass than I did on rock. My boots gripped the rock firmly, but the grassy slopes were sometimes slippery.

As we edged around the southwestern part of the snowfield we came to a steep icy couloir. It was perhaps only twenty feet across, but it plunged down the face for hundreds of feet. I slipped my ice ax off my backpack while Jon carefully set up a belay for me, and then made my way across the couloir, cutting steps as I did so. Once across this delicate traverse, I belayed Jon across. We continued following the ledge around the snowfield for another few hundred feet, before scrambling across the rock that separated the two snowfields.

When we reached the second and higher of the two snowfields, I was surprised to see how steep it was. In the pictures I had taken of Mt. Owen from the Grand the snowfield didn't appear to be very steep, nor did it appear so from Jackson Hole.

Jon waited comfortably in the bergschrund while I proceeded the length of a rope to a belay point. We proceeded in this fashion for three or four rope lengths until we came to the top of the upper snowfield. Leaving our ice axes there, we scrambled up rocky slabs through a large gully for several hundred feet. I regret the fact that we didn't take more time to study the surroundings, but I had only one goal in mind, that of reaching the summit, so we moved right along.

Still high above, a huge overhanging rock blocked the route to the summit. We climbed under this rock, and then proceeded up a vertical chimney for about forty feet. Climbing was tricky near the top. Three or four easier pitches led to a broad ledge on which we traversed across the northwest face of the mountain. The exposure here was terrific, nearly three thousand vertical feet, but the view was breathtaking!

Climbing above the ledge, we entered a very deep chimney. As I came to the top of it, I looked around expecting to see another rock wall towering above. What a pleasant surprise when I saw nothing but a small platform that sloped up perhaps twenty feet to the north. We were on the summit!

What a joy it was for me! A dream of some twenty-five years to climb all the major Teton peaks had become a reality!

Once on the summit, we unroped, but walked around very cautiously. The summit of Mt. Owen was interesting. The highest part of the summit rises to the north about ten feet above the rest of the summit block. A narrow ridge perhaps only three feet wide with several humps leads to it. The exposure to the west and north was incredible; the mountain just falls away into the abyss below.

The southern part of the summit was roomier; it was perhaps eight feet long from east to west and five feet wide. Unlike most of the other Teton peaks, which consist of large broken rock, the summit of Owen consisted of a hard cap.

The view was spectacular! The sky was clear; there didn't appear to be a cloud in the sky. To the south the North Face of the Grand dominated the scene. No matter from which peak one looks at the Grand, it always towers so much higher above. In this case the Grand rose still another 848 feet above us.

To the west of the Grand, the Enclosure rose to 13,000 feet.

Looking to the southeast, the Teton Glacier, where we had spent the night, and Delta, Amphitheater, and Surprise lakes seemed to be so far below, and beyond them another three thousand feet lower lay Taggart and Bradley lakes. As I looked down on the glacier and the boulder field where we had spent the night, I wished we were already there and thought how good I would feel when we had descended to the glacier.

FATHER JOSEPH A. MIKSCH

To the east rose the jagged pinnacles of Teewinot. To the northeast rose Mt. St. John, and farther to the north was Mt. Moran. We were three hundred feet higher than Moran. I recalled looking toward Owen from Moran two summers earlier; how grand it was to look back at it now from the summit of Owen!

I took a series of pictures in all directions. Unfortunately I was unaccustomed to using the camera, which I had only recently purchased and double-exposed several pictures.

Jon rested while I opened my daypack and ate some Bakers Sweet Chocolate and a can of fruit.

For perhaps fifteen minutes we rested; then I asked Jon if he would take several pictures of me. Gingerly I walked up the narrow, humpy ridge to the summit and stood there while Jon took several pictures. He seemed to be having some problems with the camera, however, and wasn't sure the film was advancing. Rather than take a chance of not getting some pictures from the summit, I replaced the film with another roll, and then gave Jon another brief lesson on how to operate the camera.

Neither of us had a watch, but judging from the angle of the sun, I would guess that we arrived at the summit around 10:00 a.m. and spent from fifteen to thirty minutes on the summit. All too soon it was time to head back down.

I slipped on my daypack and roped up. Jon set up a belay as I descended into the chimney. It was a large chimney, nearly the size of a room, but it had a good system of cracks and handholds. Several pitches below it and we were on the ledge overlooking the northwest face. Traversing the ledge to the south, we descended more difficult pitches and the vertical chimney. It proved to be a difficult and tricky descent. I always had the security of a rope belay, but Jon had to down climb it without protection.

Once down the difficult sections we scrambled down the gully to the top of the upper snowfield where we had left our ice axes. We traversed across the snowfield together for a ways until we came to the steep section. Jon set up a belay from a bergschrund and then told me to follow the upper edge of the snowfield for a rope's length to a place where I could get into the bergschrund and belay him across. I proceeded very cautiously, not daring to look down, but concentrating on my every step. Once I reached the bergschrund and was securely based, I took a picture looking down the snowfield and out over the Teton Glacier below. "Once down on that glacier," I thought, "and we'll be home free." But oh! What a long ways we still had to go!

Several more rope lengths and we were off the first snowfield and scrambling down the rocky ridge that separates the upper snowfields.

We unroped and climbed down to the ramp, circling around the southwestern edge of the snowfield.

When we came to the icy couloir, we roped up again in order to belay each other across the couloir; then we unroped and followed the ramp carefully around the snowfield to the Great Chimney. En route we again climbed up and down ridges and grassy slopes. Whenever we stopped the view was magnificent!

Coming to the chimney with the waterfall, we rappelled about sixty feet, taking on a little more water than I would have liked from the waterfall. Belaying each other down the remainder of the chimney to the snowfield that extended up from the col between the East Ridge and East Prong, we descended rather quickly for several rope lengths, and then traversed to the south to get to the crest of the snow and eventually were able to walk down to the col.

After walking around a bit, we left the snowfield to get our bearings before we started to descend the rocky ledges to the west of the couloir. We could walk some distance together at times, descending over easy ledges and scrambling down rocks before coming to pitches over which we needed to belay each other.

On one such pitch where I was down climbing vertical rock, I found myself clinging to a rock that bulged outward. I tried for what seemed like a long time to find a foot—or handhold, but could find nothing. Finally, I just said the heck with it and let go. Jon had a good belay on me, so I just slid down the face of the rock for about twelve feet to a place where I could get a good foothold. I would have loved to have watched Jon down climb that section, but I moved farther down and could not see him.

I no longer remember how many pitches we descended, but there were many. Most were not too difficult. As a matter of fact, some were rather enjoyable and challenging. Still, as I looked down on the glacier below, I kept thinking how great I would feel when we finally descended that last snowfield and were walking toward the boulder field where we had bivouacked overnight. We still had such a long ways to go!

As we were ascending and descending, I estimated our elevation by looking across the glacier toward prominent peaks and features whose altitudes I knew. On the East Ridge of the Grand are several prominent towers, one of which really caught my eye. It looked like a giant tooth and was so named, the "Molar Tooth." Its elevation was twelve thousand feet.

Disappointment Peak, reaching up to 11,616 feet, served as another measuring stick, and the East Prong rose above us to the east of the couloir to 12,050 feet. By considering our position in relation to these peaks, I was able to estimate our altitude fairly accurately and realized that we still had a long ways to descend.

The final three pitches down the rock wall were long ones. Usually I would down climb almost the entire rope length. Several pitches required the use of lieback moves down a vertical crack.

Once down the final pitch we walked over loose rock to the edge of the snow couloir where Jon set up a belay. He would either use a loop of nylon webbing, which he would slip around a large rock, or he would use several stoppers. Clipping a carabiner into these, he would clip into a loop he tied into his rope next to him, and then would take in the entire length of rope between him and me, making sure it was not tangled. Once he had done all this, he would belay me in the traditional fashion, feeding out the rope as I moved away.

It was psychologically unnerving to leave the security of the rock for the more exposed, steep snowfield. Descending the snow couloir into the bergschrund at the base of the rock, I belayed Jon as he climbed down.

Below the bergschrund the couloir descended steeply onto the bench, and then funneled into the gully leading down to the rotten rock band near the base of the couloir.

The band of rock turned out to be much steeper and longer than I had remembered. We still looked down on the glacier some four hundred feet below. The rock was brittle, broken, and slivery. By the time we had reached the bottom, my fingers were cut and shredded.

We descended three very long pitches of nearly vertical rock before the angle of incline began to dampen out. Upon reaching the top of the snow alluvial fan, I let out a shout for joy. The difficult part of the climb was now over. Ahead lay several traverses over icy snowfields and a long hike down to the car. My dream of climbing all the major peaks in the Teton Range had finally been accomplished.

FATHER JOSEPH A. MIKSCH

WHY DID HE?

R ECENTLY, WHILE TEACHING a scripture course to a group of sixth graders, we read chapter 22 of the book of Genesis in which God told Abraham to sacrifice his only son Isaac. Some of the students were horrified at the thought of Abraham sacrificing his son, and one yelled out: "How could God, who is so good and who loves us so much, ask poor Abraham to sacrifice his only son like that?"

I remember asking that same question fifty-eight years ago when I was in grade school.

Our teacher, a saintly Franciscan sister, who seemed to be old enough to have known Abraham personally, answered as many had before and since: "God knew all along that Abraham wouldn't have to sacrifice his son. God was merely testing Abraham to see how much he loved Him."

While such an answer may have satisfied some, it didn't do much for me. God is supposed to know everything, so why did He have to test poor Abraham! Didn't He know Abraham would be faithful? And even if God knew that Abraham wouldn't have to sacrifice his son Isaac, wasn't God putting poor Abraham through a lot of needless grief and anguish?

And what about poor Isaac! The poor boy must have been traumatized for the rest of his life! In today's society Isaac could have hired a lawyer, sued Abraham for the mental and emotional anguish he had caused him, and taken him to the cleaners!

Nope! It never made sense to me! How could a good and loving God put poor Abraham and Isaac through all that!

The account in Genesis reminds me of the time when a missionary priest from Africa came to the parish where I was serving as an associate pastor to make an appeal for assistance. The pastor had taken a week's vacation, so I had the rectory to myself. I wasn't much of a housekeeper. Dirty dishes had piled up in the kitchen, and the house was a mess, so on Saturday morning I decided to clean up a bit before the missionary arrived.

I was busily stacking dirty dishes on the counter by the sink and putting things down the garbage disposal. While working at the table, the vibration of the garbage disposal caused the silverware to slide off the counter and down into the disposal. It was a powerful machine, which soon filled the air with flying bits of shrapnel. Fearing for my life, I ducked under the table. The plan was to use the table as a shield as I crept toward the switch to turn off the disposal.

Just after crawling under the table I became aware of a pair of black slacks and shoes standing by the door; the missionary had arrived. I yelled to him to take cover, and then proceeded toward the sink to turn off the disposal. Somewhat embarrassed, I crawled out from under the table and introduced myself to my guest.

I have often wondered what that missionary must have thought as he witnessed that comic scene and what tales he must have told the people in Africa about the strange things people in America do.

The reason why I remember this incident in conjunction with the story of Abraham and Isaac is because of what the missionary told us that weekend. He told us that the people in Africa where he worked were a very religious people. Before the missionaries came, they worshipped the gods and lived in constant fear of evil spirits. They spent a long time each day in prayer and chants, shaking rattles to ward off the evil spirits. In time of natural disasters, such as droughts, they would sacrifice much of their meager possessions in an attempt to appease the gods or placate the evil spirits. It wasn't uncommon, for example, for a man with only three or four cows to slaughter one of them and offer it in sacrifice. All the while the people lived in fear of the gods or worried about making the evil spirits angry.

What a joy it was for missionaries to come to these people and tell them that they didn't have to live in fear of the gods or evil spirits! There was only one God and He was a God of love. He didn't demand huge sacrifices. All He wanted them to do was to believe in His Son Jesus who came to teach us to love God above all else and to love one another. What a joy, what a relief it was for these people to hear the "Good News"!

As I listened to his story about the people of Africa, I thought of Abraham and his contemporaries. They were probably very much like the people of Africa to whom this missionary ministered. They believed in many gods, and probably in evil spirits. In an effort to appease the gods, they were willing to offer great sacrifices. They were even willing to offer their most priceless possessions, their children, in human sacrifice.

It wasn't because they were cruel, sadistic people that they offered human sacrifice. Quite the contrary, they loved their children! They valued children perhaps more than we do today. They lived in societies in which there were no welfare programs, no retirement benefits, and no social security system to provide for their needs in their old age. Their children would look after them and provide security for them in their old age.

They had no concept of an afterlife, a heaven, or life beyond the grave. The only way they could hope to achieve some sense of immortality was through the memory of their children and grandchildren.

Thus, for these people to have children, a large family, was their main goal in life. Children would provide for them in their old age; they could live on after death in the memory of their children. To be childless was considered to be a curse.

They lived in such fear, awe, and reverence for their gods, however, that they were willing to offer up their firstborn, their most priceless possession, in sacrifice to appease the gods.

Abraham was a man of his times. He was familiar with the practice of his contemporaries to offer human sacrifice and thus he too was willing to offer up his only son Isaac. He was about to do so when God revealed to him that such sacrifice was not necessary. The God of Abraham did not demand human sacrifice! Because of this revelation, which God made to Abraham, his descendants, the Israelites, later found the notion of human sacrifice abhorrent. Through Abraham, and later through Moses and the prophets, God revealed to His people that He does not ask us to do difficult things. He doesn't need our sacrifices, rather He simply wants us to do what common sense tells us to do anyway, to love God above all things and to love one another.

What I find so interesting as I reflect upon the story of Abraham and Isaac is that what God does not demand of Abraham or any of us, He Himself was willing to do for us! He sent His Son to live among us and allowed Him to be sacrificed on the cross for our salvation. How incredible!

Now when I reflect upon this story in the book of Genesis, I no longer ask the question: "How could God ask Abraham to do such a thing?" Rather I'm filled with a sense of wonder and awe over the fact that God loved us so much that He sacrificed His only Son for our salvation. Overwhelmed by the mystery, I can only ask in wonder: "Why did He?"

THE FAITH WE TAKE FOR GRANTED

I WAS SITTING in a car parked along a busy street, waiting for my mother who was still doing some shopping. It was a hot and humid day, and I was becoming rather impatient. I didn't care for the noise on the radio. I had brought no books along to read, and thus I was just plain bored! Then I saw a man walking down the sidewalk and coming toward me. He was an elderly fellow. He wore dark sunglasses and was tapping the edge of the sidewalk with a long white cane. I watched the blind man as he walked by; with his cane he discovered every obstacle, doorway, and dip in the sidewalk. He came to the end of the block, paused momentarily, and then slowly proceeded across the street as traffic stopped for him. Soon he disappeared around the corner.

I continued to sit in the car waiting for my mother, but I was no longer restless or bored. I was lost in thought and prayer. I suddenly realized how wonderful it is to be able to see. Such a grand and tremendous gift and I had taken it so much for granted. I spent the rest of my "waiting time" in prayer, thanking God for the gift of sight and praying for the blind man and for all who are sightless. I've reflected back on that brief scene often and continue to thank God frequently for the gift of sight. I've often thought too that that blind man's cross, his blindness, is God's special gift to the rest of us. His blindness makes countless others appreciate their gift of sight. His mere presence speaks louder and more powerfully than the best prepared sermon or homily.

Just as I came to appreciate the gift of sight so much the more because of that blind man, I have come to appreciate the gift of faith so much the more because of an experience I had with a man who had no faith. Growing up Catholic from infancy, I took my faith pretty much for granted. It was an important part of my upbringing; I went through all the motions and at times truly felt "touched by God." Still, I don't think I truly appreciated what a difference my faith made until I first came to know someone who did not believe in God, an afterlife, or anything.

His name was Gerard. He was one of the chief foremen and often served as our backpacker back in the days when I was working for the Department of the Interior in one of our national parks. Working on trails in the backcountry of the park, we would hike into the backcountry for a five—or ten-day stretch to set up camp and work on the trails in the area. Our food and supplies would be hauled on horseback in a pack train. Gerard was a cowboy and woodsman who came right out of TV's *Gun Smoke* or one of Zane Gray's novels. He knew the backcountry like no one else I have ever met. Often when trekking through the mountains or canyons, Gerard would stop and begin to grin. We knew he had spotted something, but nothing could we see. After a few minutes Gerard would point toward a grove of trees, but still we could see nothing. Then he would say: "Over there, see it, a moose's ear." Five minutes later we would finally spot the critter as it moved in the underbrush, but Gerard had spotted that moose from half a mile away.

As the hunting season was approaching, hunters were eagerly awaiting the opening day, dreaming of the trophy they would bring home. When the season would finally open, they would all be up and gone at the crack of dawn, but Gerard would saunter around until 9:00 or 10:00 a.m. before leaving park headquarters. By noon he would be back with the first elk or deer, and usually it was one of the larger critters taken in the hunt.

Gerard's pride and joy was his eleven-year-old son. As we sat around our backcountry campfire in the evenings, he was all Gerard would talk about. He would tell us how good his son could ride a horse, lead it across a rock slide, how straight he could shoot, rope a calf, or read the signs left by wild game along a trail. That boy was Gerard's pride and joy, and he was going to teach him every skill he knew.

I was only a seasonal employee at the park, working there from Memorial Day till Labor Day. When I reported back to work for my third summer early in June, I met Gerard in the office. Ever before we shook hands I knew that something was wrong. Gerard just wasn't the man I had known him to be the previous summer.

His smile wasn't quite the same, and the sparkle had gone out of his eyes. I soon learned from others that his son was terminally ill with a rare form of cancer. The little boy died in mid-July.

His funeral was the saddest I have ever attended. Gerard and his family had no faith. They belonged to no church; Jesus was unknown to them. For them there was no "Good News." Their son, their pride and joy, had died. He would be forever gone, and someday they too would follow him into oblivion. We went to the mortuary, but no prayers were said. We expressed our condolences, and then stood in mute silence.

The next morning we drove from the mortuary to the cemetery. No cemetery I have ever visited was as barren and desolate as that rocky, sagebrush-covered Wyoming cemetery. The casket was carried from the hearse and placed over the opened grave. We all stood there in silence for a few minutes; then one by one we filed past, shook hands with Gerard, his wife, and family, and walked away. I have never felt so empty, so helpless or sad. I wanted to cry out: "Gerard, this isn't the end! There's much, much more! Jesus has come to give us eternal life! Your son is not alone! He is fully alive with God in heaven and you shall be reunited with him again someday." But Gerard and his family didn't share those beliefs, so I said nothing.

I will never forget that funeral though. I know now, more than I had ever known before, just how much my faith in Jesus means and what a difference it makes in the way I look at life. I can't imagine what life would be like without faith in Jesus. Without such faith life would be so empty, and death would come with such awful finality. Because of our faith in Jesus, even death makes sense and is cause for rejoicing.

I pray often for people like Gerard and his family who have no faith that they may someday come to believe, and I thank God for men like Gerard who taught me to appreciate that tremendous gift, which I so often take for grant, the gift of my Catholic faith.

Years ago when I was in grade school and we were encouraged to pray for the success of the missionary efforts of the church, I used to think of people in distant lands who had not yet heard the "Good News." I still think of them today as I pray for the missions, but I also think of people like Gerard whom I knew personally, and friends and neighbors who may live in the house next door, who do not yet believe. We all know people like this, many of whom are hungering for meaning and purpose in life. I know from my experience with the RCIA program in our parish that many are just waiting for someone to extend an invitation to them to "come and see" what we have to offer. If we extend that invitation, they too may one day be able to appreciate the great gift of our Catholic faith!

THE HOLY SPIRIT AT WORK IN OUR MIDST

I OFTEN WONDER what thoughts must have been going through Peter's mind on the evening of the first Pentecost.

Perhaps he was thinking: "Did this day really happen? Did I really preach with such enthusiasm to all those people? Shy, timid me? Not so long ago I didn't have the courage even to admit to a servant girl that I was a companion of Jesus. *Wow!*"

As a newly ordained priest, I used to wonder why we don't see similar manifestations of the Spirit in our own day and age. After all, we do believe that when we are confirmed, we receive the same gifts of the Holy Spirit that Peter and the other apostles received. So why don't we see a similar response to the Holy Spirit's presence as did the apostles that first Pentecost?

I'm quite a bit older now, and I've had an opportunity to observe people for many years. And I am absolutely convinced that the Holy Spirit is present in our world today, and that He will touch each of us at some time in our lives and place His gifts upon us! When that happens, look out! If we respond to the promptings of the Holy Spirit, incredible things will happen!

One of my duties over the years has been that of teaching in high schools. At first I didn't find teaching to be very rewarding. Even students who did well in my classes soon seemed to forget everything I had taught them. At times I felt like a failure. I began to question whether I was in the right profession.

And then it happened! I began to see the presence of the Holy Spirit at work among my students! Was I ever in for a surprise!

It all began with the "worst student" I had ever taught. Every teacher has one or two of them. This boy was impossible. He was big for a high school freshman—six foot tall and weighed 180 pounds. He came to class when he felt like it and left when he became bored. God alone knew where his textbooks were—he certainly didn't. He never bothered with homework. When he came to class, we teachers hoped he would daydream rather than cause a disturbance. He didn't attend Mass on Sunday, mouthed off to teachers, and refused to greet us when we met in the corridor or in the street. He caused his parents just as much grief at home. They didn't know what to do with him either.

We put up with his behavior throughout his freshman year, but midway through his sophomore year the faculty and administration voted unanimously to expel him. We were unable to help him and believed his presence was detrimental to the rest of the student body.

I can still remember so vividly the morning he left school for the last time. I stood in the office and watched as he walked out the front door. I felt very bad. I felt as though we had failed him, though I knew we had done everything we could in an effort to get through to him. I also remember thinking that day: "There goes a young man for whom the church will never have any meaning."

A spirit of peace seemed to prevail after his dismissal. Faculty members felt a certain tension had been lifted from them, and the overall discipline in the school seemed to improve. We still had to contend with his girlfriend who shared his negative attitude. We did manage to cope with her and were delighted to see her graduate.

With the passage of time I almost forgot about these two students. The only time, in fact, that I thought of them was when I would hear another teacher mention the "worst student" he or she had ever taught.

Some years later, when my schedule permitted, I decided to become active in the Cursillo Movement again. When I walked into the kitchen area during one of the Cursillo weekends, I was startled. There was the boy, now a grown man, whom we had kicked out of school. I walked up to him and shook his hand.

"Chuck," I said, "what in the world are you doing here? The penitentiary! Death row! Yes! But not here! This is the last place in the world I would expect to find you!" He smiled.

"Father Joe," he said, "I've participated in every one of these weekends for the past five years."

I was speechless as he went on to tell me that his wife, who as a young woman also had given us trouble, was the director of this particular women's weekend.

Later I saw Chuck's mother and expressed my surprise at seeing her son on the weekend and hearing of his involvement in the movement.

"Oh, Father Joe," she said, "you know what a difficult time we had with him when he was growing up. We didn't know what to do with him anymore. And now we sit around the dining room table with our Bibles, reading and talking about Jesus. God is so good! If someone would have told me this would happen, I never would have believed it."

She then went on to tell me how involved her son and daughter-in-law were in their parish—serving as extraordinary ministers of the Eucharist and taking Holy Communion to shut-ins, teaching high school students in the CCD program, serving as lectors, and on the parish council. They were now one of the most active couples in their parish—the young man for whom I had thought the church would never have any meaning. I learned an important lesson that day: When the Holy Spirit touches someone, look out! Incredible things can happen!

Then there was Brenda, a poor student who couldn't seem to concentrate and often slept through my classes. I stopped by her home one night around 9:30 p.m. unannounced and was invited to join the family for dinner. I learned that this was the usual time for dinner. I also learned why Brenda often slept through my class and was doing so poorly scholastically. She helped with the chores on the farm each night until late in the evening and also early in the morning before going to school. She was tired and had little time to study.

Somehow she managed to get through school and graduated. Several years later she introduced me to her fiancé whom I had the privilege of instructing and bringing into the Catholic faith. A few months after they were married, I was transferred to another parish. A year or two later I received the joyful news that they had become parents.

Some weeks later I learned that their baby had a rare terminal illness and wasn't expected to live beyond age two, so l went to visit them and express my concern and assure them of my support.

That visit turned out to be one of the most inspiring moments of my life. Her husband was at work, so I visited with Brenda and her child. I was so deeply impressed by the way this woman showed her love for her child. Tears were streaming down my face as I drove home that night, so moved was I by the love that mother showed for that baby.

I made a point of visiting her several times during the months that followed. As the child's illness progressed, and more and longer hospital stays were required, the young woman joined a charismatic prayer group at the hospital and truly was touched by the Holy Spirit. She began to share her faith with everyone, reading and talking about the scriptures. After a visit with her I would find myself driving away filled with admiration and awe for her simple, but deep faith, wondering whether this really was the girl who used to sleep through my religion class.

When the baby died, there wasn't a dry eye in church as people came forward to view that tiny body, dressed in white, in a little casket. But Brenda was radiant. Through the power of the Holy Spirit, she knew beyond doubt that God had welcomed a new saint into heaven!

Some months later the phone rang early one morning. I picked up the receiver and recognized the distraught voice of this young woman's father. He told me she had just been killed in an auto accident. Even today, I often think of this beautiful young mother with tears in my eyes, and I thank God for the beautiful lessons she taught me about a mother's love for her child, about faith and life, and realize once again that when the Holy Spirit touches one, incredible things can happen!

I remember Germaine, mother of a large family, whose husband was afflicted with a cancerous brain tumor at the age of forty-eight, and how she cared for him at home so faithfully during the final two years of his life, while at the same time preparing for a son's wedding and participating actively in all the school activities of her younger children.

When he was no longer able to walk, she would bring him to daily Mass in a wheelchair. I recall seeing her pushing his wheelchair through the snow one wintry Sunday morning, the wheels clogged with snow. Their car had broken down some distance from church, so she pushed him through the snow for several blocks. After a lecture about the need to use better judgment on such a blizzardly day, I assured her that I would be more than happy to come to their home to celebrate the Eucharist, and then stepped back in silent admiration and wonder at this woman's deep faith and her love for God and for her husband. Truly the Holy Spirit had touched her. She was an inspiration to all the members of her community.

I often think of Jon and Vicki! When they came to talk to me about getting married, I tried to discourage them; I felt they were too young. They did marry, however, and God soon blessed them with a beautiful daughter, and then a son.

Some years later, while visiting the hospital, I stepped into an elevator; Jon stepped in right behind me. He greeted me with a big smile. In one hand he held a box of candy, and in the other he had several long-stemmed roses. His wife had just given birth to another son. It truly did my heart good to see the obvious joy and pride that Jon felt.

The next day I received a call from Jon's grandmother. She wanted to know if I could visit Jon and Vicki. They had just learned that their little boy had Down syndrome.

My visit with the young couple was subdued. There were no smiles now, only worried looks and long periods of silence. It was such devastating news! Although they had not raised the question, as I drove home after our visit, I couldn't help but wonder why God permits such things to happen to a young couple so willing and ready to accept children when so many others choose to abort their healthy babies.

The months ahead were difficult for Jon and Vicki. Like so many children with Down syndrome, their son's heart needed repair, but he was too weak and feeble to undergo surgery. He had to be fed through a tube in his nose and Vicki had to learn quickly to become a nurse.

After seven long months surgery finally was possible. I was privileged to spend several hours with Jon and Vicki and their family in the hospital during the seemingly endless four-hour surgery. Tension and worry clearly were written across their faces. I watched carefully when the doctor came in to brief them after the operation and told them that it had gone better than expected. I could see the tension ease from their faces, and I realized more than ever how much they loved that little child. At that moment I realized why God permitted such a tragedy to befall this couple. They were a couple who could accept such child with unconditional love.

Jon and Vicki's son is now a young man, confined to a wheelchair, unable to speak more than a few words, and is fed through a tube in his stomach. Watching his parents, and older brother and sister, taking care of him is an inspiration to me and the entire community, and just one more beautiful example of the Holy Spirit at work in our midst.

Then there is Carl! Years ago, as a junior in high school, he was in my religion class. A pleasant fellow with an outgoing personality, a born leader, and a good student, Carl loved having a good time and managed to make it to every party in town. After graduation, he went into the military and became a heavy equipment operator; then he went on to get his degree in mechanical engineering.

One evening, while attending Mass in the church just across the street from the college campus, the pastor in his homily told those present that they needed to do more than just pray for vocations to the priesthood and religious life; then to the young adults present, he said, "Some of you have to answer God's call!"

That's when the Holy Spirit touched Carl. He took that message to heart and five years later was ordained to the priesthood.

Talk about a surprise! Carl a priest? I would never have guessed it when I taught him as a junior in high school. Today I couldn't be more proud of him and the work he is doing with the help of the Holy Spirit!

I think of Don and Nancy, whose second child, Paul, was severely and profoundly retarded because of a rare genetic disease, fucosidosis. Although he was twenty-five years old, he looked like a boy of ten and never uttered a word in his entire life. While his parents could have put him into an institution where he would have been cared for, they had chosen instead to put him in a nearby regional school where he could receive therapy and spend weekends at home with them. Thus, every weekend, Don and Nancy could be seen taking care of their son, wheeling him about outside when the weather permitted, bringing him to Mass on Sunday, and setting a beautiful example of unconditional parental love for all the members of their parish and community.

The Holy Spirit was obviously at work on that first Pentecost when Peter and the apostles were inspired to go forth and proclaim the "Good News." That same Holy Spirit continues to be present in our lives today. All we need to do is look around, and we will see evidence of that!

When I conduct retreats and work with young adults who are preparing to receive the gifts of the Holy Spirit through the reception of the sacrament of confirmation, I share with them my memories of Chuck, Brenda, Carl, and others, and how the Holy Spirit touched them. I tell them how excited I am about their reception of the sacrament of confirmation because I know that someday the Holy Spirit will touch them too, and when He does, great things will happen if they cooperate with Him. And I say this with absolute conviction, for it is Jesus who promises to send the Holy Spirit, and He keeps His promises!

Indeed, we do live in the age of the Spirit! The Holy Spirit inspired a conclave of cardinals on October 28, 1958, to elect Angelo Roncalli, who, it was thought, would be a do-nothing pope; but as Pope John XXIII, he was led by the Spirit to call the Second Vatican Council. We see the manifestations of the Holy Spirit in the work of such saintly people as Mother Teresa of Calcutta and John Paul II. We see the Holy Spirit at work in movements such as Cursillo, Marriage Encounter, Beginning Experience, Search, and TEC for young people. It is the presence of the Spirit that enables us to use our talents and abilities to serve others in our local communities, or gives us the grace and strength to care for a sick or handicapped child.

Jesus promised to send the Holy Spirit upon us, and He will be faithful to the promise! Only God knows how and when each of us will be touched by the Spirit, but when we are, look out! Incredible things can happen!

THE HEALING POWER OF JESUS

WHEN I WAS a young priest, I went to the hospital to visit an uncle who was seriously ill and extremely depressed. He talked to those of us who were there about death, giving us final instructions on how to dispose of some of his belongings. When I left the hospital that Sunday night to return to my parish, I thought I was saying good-bye to him for the last time.

I fully expected to receive a call during the night or the next day to inform me that he had died. But no call came on Monday or Tuesday. By Wednesday I couldn't stand the tension any longer, so I called home to inquire about his condition. Much to my surprise, I was told he was doing much better.

When I went to visit him on Thursday, I couldn't believe how much he had improved. He was sitting up in a chair, eating solid food, and talking about going home. He was released shortly thereafter and lived on his own for several years.

During the course of our visit and many times thereafter, he spoke repeatedly about what had happened late that Sunday evening after I had left the hospital. Around midnight an elderly nun came to his room to pray with him—she regularly visited those who were near death. She prayed with him and read the account of Jesus curing the leper (Mark 1:40-45). She told him, "You are no better or worse than that leper! Jesus can cure you too, if you ask him." With such words of encouragement, she continued to pray with him for a short time.

"From that very moment," my uncle said, "I knew I was going to get better."

Did that nun have the power of healing? I don't know! Would my uncle have died if she had not come to visit him? I don't know, but I do know that she had helped change his attitude from depression and despair to hope. Perhaps that was all he needed to regain his physical strength.

To understand the importance of healing in the ministry of Jesus and of the early church, we need to comprehend the Jewish attitude toward sickness, suffering, and death at the time of Jesus. John's Gospel recalls the time when Jesus and his disciples saw a man who was blind from birth. The disciples asked if the blindness was due to the blind man's sin or that of his parents. Jesus answered, "Neither he nor his parents sinned; it is so that the works of God might be made visible through him" (9:3). Although Jesus made it very clear that sickness cannot be considered a punishment suffered for personal sins, such an attitude was prevalent during His time.

But Jesus came to restore grace, that relationship between God and human beings which was lost through original sin. He came to destroy the power of Satan over us. Thus, by recording Jesus's healing miracles the evangelists point out that the power of Satan is being broken. Even Satan's mightiest weapon—death—is rendered powerless by Jesus, who raised the daughter of Jairus (Mark 5:21-24, 35-43), the widow's son at Naim (Luke 7:11-17), and Lazarus (John 11:1-44), and then rose gloriously from the dead himself.

Thus, when the disciples of John the Baptist are sent to Jesus to ask whether he might be the Messiah, he tells them, "Go and tell John what you have seen and heard: the blind regain their sight, the lame walk, lepers are cleansed, the deaf hear, the dead are raised, the poor have the good news proclaimed to them" (Luke 7:22).

These healing actions of Jesus speak for themselves. They proclaim the dawn of the messianic age—the Kingdom of God is at hand. "He summoned the Twelve and gave them power and authority over all demons and to cure diseases, and he sent them to proclaim the kingdom of God and to heal [the sick]" (Luke 9:1-2).

No one would question the importance of the healing ministry of Jesus or that of the early church, but people often feel uncomfortable when we speak of healing as a ministry in the church today. After all, that's the realm of the medical profession. If we speak of healing, we tend to feel more comfortable speaking in terms of "spiritual" healing or "psychological" healing—peace of mind.

Perhaps we should avoid making such distinctions. Is a physically ill person more ill than someone who is physically well, but mentally or emotionally ill? Hasn't healing taken place if someone gains peace of mind through the reception of the sacrament of anointing?

We need to think in terms of a holistic approach to healing, one which includes psychological, emotional, and spiritual dimensions. Psychosomatic illnesses are physical illnesses that are psychologically induced. We know that stress and worry can lead to ulcers and heart attacks. Our mental attitude has been proven to be very important in overcoming illness. Sometimes one's attitude can be the determining factor as to whether one will recover or succumb to an illness.

Jesus continues to heal us today through the sacrament of anointing the sick. That healing may be spiritual or psychological. Sometimes, in a very dramatic way, it may be physical.

On one occasion I went to visit a parishioner who had several bouts with cancerous tumors in her throat. She had surgery and chemo treatments, but the tumors came back. After an examination by her local doctor, she was scheduled to see her specialist in a distant city. The day before her appointment, I dropped by to visit her. We prayed together. I anointed her and gave her Holy Communion.

As I placed my hands upon her head during the rite of anointing, I prayed with all my heart that, if it be God's will, Jesus touch her with His healing power.

When she returned from her visit to the specialist, I again dropped by for a visit, expecting to hear some bad news. Instead I found a woman who was up and about, full of energy and filled with joy. "Father Joe," she said, "it's a miracle!"

She then proceeded to tell me that after she had been anointed, she had the most wonderful night's sleep. She felt so very much at peace and just seemed to know that everything was going to be all right. Next day, when she walked into the doctor's office, before she could say anything, the doctor said to her, "I had this strange feeling this morning that when you came in for your examination, I would find no trace of your cancer." He then went on to examine her, using all sorts of instruments, which he ran down her throat. When he was finished, he just shook his head and said, "I just don't understand it. There are no signs of cancer. The tumors are all gone."

It has been four or five years since then, and she continues to be cancer-free. Medical science can't explain how such things can happen. She doesn't need a scientific explanation. She knows that Jesus touched and healed her through the sacrament of the anointing of the sick.

I do believe that Jesus sometimes chooses to exercise his healing power in dramatic ways through this sacrament. When He chooses to do so through me, I can only step back in fear, wonder, and awe, and marvel over the fact that Jesus would elect to work such wonders through a sinful instrument like me.

In recent years I have become aware of another dimension to this sacrament. Whenever I anoint someone, I refer to this passage from Paul's letter to the Colossians (1:24):

Now I rejoice in my sufferings for your sake,
and in my flesh I am filling up what is lacking
in the afflictions of Christ on behalf of his body,
which is the Church.

I point out that the purpose of the sacrament of the sick is twofold: It is the church's sacrament of healing through which we truly believe that Jesus grants healing, which may be spiritual, psychological, or physical—maybe all three. It is also a sacrament through which the church is inviting us to unite our sufferings with the sufferings of Jesus on the cross. This enables us to share in the redemptive work of Jesus.

I then ask people who are about to be anointed to offer up their sufferings, pain, worry, and anxiety for someone who needs that special grace of conversion to return to the Lord. By so doing, people have told me that their suffering took on a new meaning and purpose. And the results have been incredible—absolutely incredible!

For example, I anointed a man who was terminally ill with cancer and asked him to offer up his sufferings for someone who needed that special grace of conversion. Less than twenty-four hours later a man appeared at my doorstep. He wanted to go to confession—he had been away for thirty-two years. After celebrating the sacrament with him, I asked him why he had chosen to come that particular day after staying away for so many years. He looked at me, shook his head, and said, "Father, I really don't know. I'm not from this area. I was driving into town and saw your sign along the highway. I suddenly felt I needed to do something to straighten out my life with God. I really don't know how to explain it."

Less than an hour later another man came to my door. He had been away for more than twenty years, and his story was almost the same. At first I thought these were just coincidences, but not anymore.

Once after I anointed a man in the hospital, a nurse approached me as I was walking out of the room and said, "Father Joe, there's a lady in room 327 who wants to see a priest." When I went to see the woman, she told me that she had been away from the church for fourteen years.

During our brief visit, she received the sacraments of reconciliation, the anointing the sick, and Holy Communion. I visited her twice more that week, but when I dropped by for a third visit, I learned she had died during the night.

FATHER JOSEPH A. MIKSCH

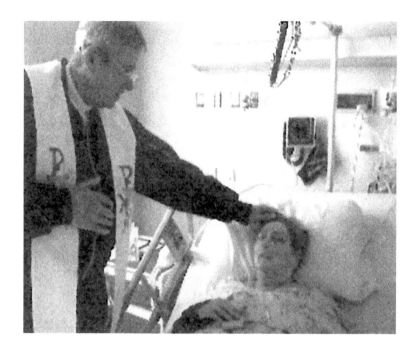

On another occasion after the morning Mass I anointed a woman who was extremely ill in the hospital. I asked her to offer up her suffering for someone who needed God's special grace of conversion.

Later that morning a young man from out of town dropped by my office to tell me that his mother was in the local community hospital. He was concerned about her since she was very ill and had been away from the sacraments for a long time. I assured him that I would visit her. He cautioned me that she might not be receptive to my visit and asked me not to tell her of his visit with me.

That afternoon I went to the hospital to visit her. When I walked into the room, her son and husband were sitting near her bed. I introduced myself. Before I could strike up a conversation, she motioned to her husband and son to leave the room, saying, "Would you please leave? I want to talk to Father alone!" She made her confession. I anointed her, and she received the Eucharist.

Several times a year I conduct a communal anointing service for the elderly members of the parish and those who are chronically ill. At one of these liturgies I anointed sixty-two individuals. Normally, I don't keep track of the number, but on this occasion I was impressed by the fact that so many came forward, so I kept track. I anointed sixty-two individuals that morning.

Later that morning, one of the individuals who took Communion to the hospital reported back to me that there was a man in the special care unit who wanted to receive the Eucharist, but he wanted to visit with a priest first. I immediately went to see him. An elderly gentleman, he had been away from the sacraments for many years and wanted to go to confession. "Bless me, Father," he began: "I've been thinking about this all morning. It must be something like sixty-two years since I last went to confession." I can still feel the hairs rising on the back of my neck as I heard his confession, knowing that I was witnessing a miracle of grace. I anointed him, game him Communion, and three days later officiated at his funeral.

Coincidence? No! I don't think so!

On another occasion a lady dropped by the rectory to be anointed before going to the hospital for surgery. She left my office at 10:00 a.m. Fifteen minutes later I received a call from another person who wanted to receive the sacrament of reconciliation. She had been away for sixteen years.

Such incidents have happened so often during the course of the past few years that I now expect someone to appear at my doorstep after I administer the sacrament of anointing the sick. I even tell people of these "coincidences" when I am about to anoint them and let them know that I will report back to them as soon as someone comes.

Through such experiences I have become aware of the communal dimensions of the sacrament of anointing the sick and the incredibly wonderful way in which God's healing power and love are extended to us. Not only does God heal the sick who are being anointed, but through their intercession, their prayers, and the uniting of their sufferings with the sufferings of Jesus on the cross, God's healing power is extended to others. And when this happens, all I can do is stand back in wonder and awe, giving praise and thanks to God for allowing me to witness miracles of His grace at work among us.

When visiting parishioners who are chronically ill, who may be confined to a wheelchair because of a stroke, I also like to remind them of the passage in John's Gospel that describes one of the postresurrection appearances of Jesus to Peter, John, and some of the other disciples (John 21:1-19). First, Jesus gives Peter a chance to make up for his threefold denial by asking him, "Simon, son of John, do you love me?" (21:16)

Then Jesus says to Peter, "I tell you solemnly: as a young man you fastened your belt and went about as you pleased; but when you are older you will stretch out your hands, and another will tie you fast and carry you off against your will" (21:18).

FATHER JOSEPH A. MIKSCH

The gospel continues: "What he said indicated the sort of death by which Peter was to glorify God" (21:19).

We know from tradition that in his old age Peter was led out and crucified in the Circus Maximus.

I remind people who have suffered a debilitating illness that when they were young, they too went about as they pleased, but now they are confined to their sick bed or wheelchair. By accepting and embracing this cross like St. Peter did, they too can glorify God.

Such an attitude can give meaning and purpose to their suffering when otherwise there may be only frustration, anger, and pain. By embracing their crosses they too can make up "what is lacking in the afflictions of Christ on behalf of his body, which is the Church" (Col. 1:24).

BEAUTIFUL HANDS

WHILE SHOPPING IN a department store one day, I got onto an elevator to go to the next floor. A mother and her four-year-old son got on behind me. As the doors were closing in front of the little boy, his mother said to him, "Watch your fingers." The little guy held his hands up in front of his face and exclaimed, "I got mine!"

Every now and then I think of that incident and hold my hands in front of my face. I certainly am glad that I can still look at my fingers and say, "I got mine." Most often we taken our hands for granted. As Labor Day rolls around each year, I sometimes invite people to look at their hands and reflect upon them.

A gesture we often use in prayer is that of folded hands.

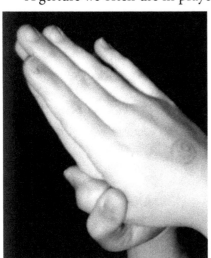

When I ask children in school why we fold our hands in prayer, most often they reply, "Because our fingers are pointing upward toward God."

Not a bad response from a child in grade school. If our fingers are pointing upward and remind us of God, I can't think of a better reason for folding our hands.

Like so many of the gestures we use in our worship, we borrowed the practice of folding our hands in prayer from secular courts. During the feudal days, AD 800-1,000 and thereabouts, the small farmers, called "serfs," often needed protection from invaders who would steal their crops and plunder their homes. So the serfs would pledge their obedience to larger landowners called "vassals" who in turn would pledge their obedience to even larger and more powerful "lords." In return for protection the serfs would have to give a large percentage of their crop to support the lords and vassals, work their land, or help build and maintain their castles. In times of danger, however, the lords and vassals would defend the serfs from invaders.

When the serf would pledge his obedience to a superior, he would kneel before him and fold his hands. The superior would place his hands over the folded hands of the serf, who would then promise his obedience and loyalty to his superior. Placing his folded hands within the hands of the superior was an act of submission; one is helpless when one's hands are squeezed between those of another person.

On the day of my ordination I knelt before my bishop at the end of Mass and folded my hands. He placed his hands over mine and asked me, "Do you promise to be obedient to me and to be my successor?" to which I responded, "I do."

Thus, the gesture of folded hands is a symbol of our pledge of obedience and submission to God, our heavenly Father. Jesus taught us to pray: "Thy will be done on earth as it is in heaven." Our prayers for whatever need should always be presented to the Father with the attitude, "Thy will be done."

Most people are familiar with the painting of Albrecht Durer called *Praying Hands*. We see it often on memorial cards or done in ceramic. There is a beautiful story about those praying hands. The story about the origin of that painting was made popular some years ago on one of the old radio dramas entitled *The Hour of Saint Francis* and is retold here with permission from Franciscan Communications.

Albrecht Durer was the son of a poor goldsmith. Unhappy with his work as an apprentice goldsmith, Albrecht went off to the city on his own to study art and drawing at one of the famous art schools. There he befriended another art student by the name of Jerome. Together they shared a tiny room, getting up early each morning to attend art school from 8:00 a.m. until 5:00 p.m. They worked in the evening from 6:00 p.m. until 1:00 or 2:00 a.m., making barely enough money to pay their rent, buy their brushes and supplies, pay their tuition, and buy a few crusts of bread. For several years they survived under these austere conditions.

Both men exhibited great artistic ability. The master artist encouraged them to spend more time on painting and to concentrate more on their work. Unfortunately they could spend no more time on painting since they had to work to support themselves. They were too exhausted to concentrate more on their work.

Finally, one evening as they were discussing their awful situation, Jerome came up with a brilliant idea. What if one of them would drop out of school and work full time; he could support the two of them while the other devoted all of his time and energies to painting. Once the one in school perfected his technique and could begin to exhibit and sell his paintings, he could support the other while he returned to school to perfect his talent. It was the idea of a genius! In this way both could achieve their goal.

Albrecht, being the younger of the two, offered to go to work first, but Jerome, recognizing Albrecht's superior talents, encouraged him to go to school first. He could perfect his technique more quickly, and thus both could achieve their goals in becoming professional painters more quickly.

The next day Albrecht went to school, devoting all of his time to painting, while Jerome went out and found other jobs scrubbing floors and doing other menial tasks. The work was hard, the hours were long, but Jerome was happy, for he realized that through his efforts both men would soon achieve their goals.

More than a year later it finally happened! Albrecht came home to their tiny room and threw a sack of gold coins on the table in front of Jerome. It was more money than the two of them had ever seen, enough to keep them both comfortably for some time. Albrecht had sold his first painting, a *Madonna*.

Jerome was now able to return to school and devote full time to painting. He soon discovered, however, that something had happened; he no longer had the delicate touch he once had. His professor used to compliment him for his fine and delicate lines; now they were harsh and bold. The professor, who used to tell him that he was one of the most promising students he had ever had, was now making him do rudimentary drawings and sketches, which normally were assigned to beginning students.

After some months of frustration Jerome sought a conference with his professor. "What's wrong with my work?" he asked. "You used to tell me that I was one of the most promising students you have ever had and now you are making me do elementary drawings."

The master artist shook his head. "Jerome," he said, "I don't know what is wrong with you. I wish I did. You used to have such talent and the potential to become a great artist. God sometimes gives one a talent to use and sometimes He gives one a talent to sacrifice. For reasons known only to Him He has asked you to sacrifice your talent. Jerome, you will never be a painter."

These words left Jerome feeling stunned and dismayed, but he knew his professor was right; he had known for some time that he had lost his touch.

That night when he arrived back at their room, Albrecht was preparing a gourmet meal to celebrate his latest triumph; he had sold another painting and would soon show several others at a major exhibition. His elation soon turned to sorrow when Jerome revealed his story.

Neither could understand what had happened until in desperation Jerome blurted out, "When I take a brush in my hand, it's as if it were a scrub mop! I just can't get it to do what my mind tells it to do."

At that Albrecht jumped to his feet and took Jerome's hands in his own. He realized at once what had happened. Those hands and fingers, which had once been so fine, so straight and smooth, were now rough. Jerome's fingers were twisted, and his knuckles were swollen.

"Oh, Jerome," he cried. "You've ruined your hands for me! Those long months of hard work, those harsh detergents, the long hours your hands were wrapped around a mop, have taken their toll. You've ruined your hands for my sake! Oh, Jerome, how can I ever repay you?"

Jerome responded firmly: "By becoming the greatest artist the world has ever known, Albrecht! Then I will be able to boast that I helped make you such!" (Albrecht Durer did, in fact, become Germany's greatest Renaissance painter.)

After a few minutes Jerome said to Albrecht, "Come on! We must eat and celebrate your latest success. You've sold another painting."

As they stood at the table, hands folded in prayer, Albrecht couldn't take his eyes off Jerome's twisted hands. Suddenly he was inspired. He told Jerome not to move, and then rushed over to set up his easel and get his sketching pencil. When Jerome asked him what he was doing, Albrecht responded, "I'm going to paint your hands as my way of proclaiming to all the world my gratitude to you for the sacrifices you've made for me. I'm going to paint your hands as a tribute to all men and women who work with their hands to support their loved ones." And thus did Albrecht Durer give the world *Praying Hands*.

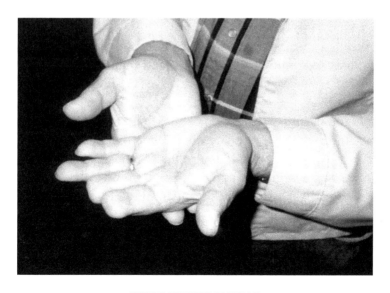

In every parish in which I have been, I have been greatly impressed by the hands of my parishioners, the hardworking hands of hardworking people—the rough, callused hands of farmers, the grease—and oil-stained hands of mechanics and machinists, the soft and loving hands of mothers with small children, the wrinkled hands of the elderly often crippled by arthritis. In every parish where I have been, I have noticed too that there are some people who can no longer hold up their hands and say like the little boy in the elevator, "I got mine." Somewhere in life's journey they have lost a finger, a thumb, and, in some cases, their entire hand. In visiting with these people I have learned that they lost those fingers or that hand while working for their loved ones. Suddenly that mangled hand becomes a beautiful proclamation of love!

I often think to myself when I see those hardworking hands, those crippled and mangled hands, that when God calls such persons from this life, when they must stand before Almighty God in judgment, they won't have to worry about their defense. All they will need to do is present their hands to the Lord, and He will embrace them in His loving arms.

One of the most beautiful gestures we now use in our liturgy is that of people presenting their open hands to receive our Lord in the Eucharist. I am often so deeply touched by the reverence with which people present their hardworking hands to receive our Lord. They come forward with open hands to receive the greatest gift a person can receive, the gift of Jesus Himself, but they certainly don't come with "empty" hands. They, too, have a gift to offer, the gift of hard work given in loving service for their families and loved ones. Jesus Himself tells us, "Whatsoever you do to the least of my brothers, that you do unto Me."

From time to time I suggest to parishioners that they hold the hands of their spouse, or those of their parents, and thank them for all the hard work they have done for you. Thank them for spending their lives in loving service of you!

I smile too when I see the hands of little children. Sometimes they are so dirty, stained with ink, dirt, and mud! Sometimes I wonder if they have ever seen a bar of soap. I'm sure my hands were just as dirty when I was a child. I'm equally sure that Jesus must be smiling when He sees those dirty hands. Their hands may be dirty, but their minds are pure and innocent.

FATHER JOSEPH A. MIKSCH

"UNLESS YOU BECOME LIKE LITTLE CHILDREN . . ."

WITH THE BEST of intentions the disciples tried to keep the little children away from Jesus, who obviously must have been tired and worn out, but He insisted: "Let the children come to me, do not hinder them! It is to such as these that the kingdom of God belongs" (Mark 10:14).

I can appreciate Jesus's love for little children; they have brought me such joy in my priestly ministry.

I recall with a smile the time our parish finance committee gave the annual "state-of-the-parish" address. The financial report was presented to the congregation on a huge screen. Halfway through the presentation I caught sight of a little four-year-old girl; she was standing in the center aisle next to her mother, totally captivated by the whole event. She didn't miss a thing. Throughout the rest of the liturgy she appeared to be deep in thought. Shortly before Communion, during one of those moments of silence, she turned to her mother and asked in a loud voice, "Are you going to give more money, Mom?"

Her startled mother nearly jumped out of the pew. Nor did I help to alleviate her embarrassment when I stopped, as I was processing down the aisle after Mass, leaned over, and asked, "Are you going to give more money?"

On another occasion, while one of the other priests was celebrating Mass, I strolled into the vestibule of the church to see if all was in order. There I met a dad who was trying to comfort his little son. The poor boy was bawling his heart out. I walked up to them and asked, "What's the matter?"

The dad looked at me in desperation and said, "Maybe you can help. He wants to know what you do with all the money the ushers just took up."

I was somewhat startled at this, but tried to explain that the money was used to pay the light and heating bill, teachers' salaries, and so forth. The little guy listened intently as he fought back tears and sniffles, but when I finished, he began to sob again and said, "I want mine back."

I assured him that many other parishioners felt the same way. I reached into my pocket to see if I had any change, but unfortunately I had none.

On another occasion I was standing by the door of the church, greeting people as they filed past, when one little fellow came up to me, hanging onto his dad's outstretched arm. Looking up at me with the brightest blue eyes, he said, "I know who you are."

"You do?" I said, fully expecting to be mistaken for Jesus as so often happens with the little ones.

"Yes!" he said with a big smile. "You helped God make me."

I quickly put up my hands to protect myself and assured his dad that I had nothing to do with it.

A missionary bishop was visiting the parish one weekend. After Mass he stood near the door of the church with me and greeted people as they filed past. A young mother stopped to visit while her little daughter looked on. She said to her daughter, "Say 'hi' to the bishop!"

She was looking right at the bishop with her back to me. Turning around, she looked up at me and said, "Hi, bishop!"

Bless her little heart. I loved that!

Little children aren't always so cute. Sometimes they can create quite a disturbance. Once as I was processing out of church after Mass, I met a dad who was standing by the doorway with his little four-year-old daughter. I greeted them and asked how they were. The father said to me, "Jill was naughty tonight. I had to take her to the back of church." Then, with a big grin, he said, "As I was carrying her back to the cry room, she said to me: 'Dad, I'd rather be whipped than be taken in with all those babies.'"

Once during the month of May we held a May crowning at one of the children's liturgies. The children processed up the aisle with such dignity as they sang "On This Day, O Beautiful Mother." All was going well until they came to the line, "Near thee, Madonna, fondly we hover." They sang: "Near the McDonald's fondly we hover."

The vision of all these dear children fondly hovering beneath the golden arches was too much for me. I burst forth with a roar of laughter.

I also find it difficult to contain myself when the little ones come to receive the sacrament of reconciliation. They pray the Act of Contrition so seriously: "Oh, my God, I'm *hardly* sorry for having *defended* Thee who *aren't* all good, and I *detest* Thy just punishments because I dread the *lost* of heaven . . . I firmly resolve with the help of *my* grace to confess my sins, to do penance and to amend my life. Amen."

The most memorable Act of Contrition that I have ever heard was prayed as follows: "Oh, my God, I am heartily sorry for all my sins which I have received from Thy bounty through Christ our Lord. Amen!" Admittedly bad theology, but prayed so sincerely I'm sure it was pleasing to the Lord.

I've also discovered that little children listen to sermons. On the Feast of the Holy Family, the second reading, taken from Paul's letter to the Colossians (3:12-21), concludes with the following statement: *"And fathers, do not nag your children lest they lose heart."*

I once concluded my homily on the Feast of the Holy Family by reminding parents not to nag their children, but to encourage them with positive strokes, compliments, and a good example. A few days later a mother called me on the phone, saying, "Father, I just wanted to call you to tell you that the five-year-olds are listening to your sermons." She went on to explain that she apparently had been pushing her five-year-old too hard to straighten up her room. Suddenly, the little girl stood her ground. Placing her hand on her hip, she looked up at her mother and said, "Mom, you didn't listen to Father Joe. He said you're not supposed to nag, and you're nagging me!"

As a priest I taught in high schools for twenty-five years and have been visiting elementary school classrooms for the past forty-three years. I have the greatest respect and appreciation for kindergarten and first-grade teachers. The longest twenty minutes of my day are those spent with the little ones! I would take high school seniors in a reform school any day.

My sister, who has taught first graders for years, once told me of the time when school was let out early because of a snowstorm. Hurriedly, she helped twenty-two little ones put on their coats, caps, scarves, mittens, and boots. The last little boy's boots were too small. She pushed, tugged, and pulled and finally got them on, only to hear the little boy say, "Sister, those aren't my boots."

Patiently biting her tongue, she proceeded to pull and tug until she got the boots off, and then asked, "Where are your boots?"

The little boy replied, "Those are my little brother's boots, but my mom said I should wear them today!"

Another teacher had a similar experience. She also pulled and tugged to get the little boy's boots on, and then asked, "Now where are your mittens?" The little boy answered, "In my boots!"

I'm sure every parent, most teachers, and many priests could relate dozens of stories like these. I suspect Jesus could tell us similar stories about the children of His day. He obviously had a deep love for children. He spoke of them often and saw in their simplicity, their humility, their openness and honesty, their confidence and trust, an example of the virtues He hoped to find in His disciples. He had these virtues in mind, I'm sure, when He said, "I assure you that whoever does not accept the reign of God like a little child shall not take part in it" (Mark 10:15).

Whenever we celebrate the sacrament of baptism in our parish, I like to share the Gospel story in which Jesus blesses the little children. In my homily I point out the virtues of little children, which we adults should try to imitate.

Little children realize their limitations. They realize that they are incapable of doing much for themselves, so they constantly come running to Mom and Dad with outstretched arms. Perhaps they are hungry, maybe they've just taken a tumble, maybe they have had a frightening experience, or a toy may need fixing. Perhaps all they need is a reassuring hug or a kiss. Whatever the need may be, they come running to Mom and Dad, arms outstretched, with complete trust and confidence in their love. In the presence of their parents there is no reason to be afraid; there they can find peace and security.

If only we adults would recognize our limitations and would remember to run to God, our Father, when we find ourselves in need. If only we would realize that we can't make it through life on our own. This is what Jesus must have had in mind when He taught us to address God as "Abba Father," as "Daddy." Like little children, we too should come running to "Abba," our "Daddy" in Heaven, with arms outstretched, with complete trust and confidence in His love. Only in His presence can we find true peace and lasting security.

I came to a deeper appreciation of the meaning of the term "Abba" one Sunday afternoon years ago when I was still a young assistant. On that particular occasion I was invited to a gathering of some of the most powerful and prominent people in the state. The governor was present, along with one of our senators from Washington, several members of Congress, the president of Union Pacific Railroad, the CEO of ConAgra, and many other leaders of the community. A simple "farm-boy" priest, I felt I was definitely out of my environment.

Keeping my mouth shut so as not to reveal my ignorance, I listened in awe as these powerful and prominent individuals discussed world economics and political issues, hanging onto every word that they uttered.

Suddenly, a little boy, perhaps four years old, came bursting into the room, ran over, and jumped into the lap of one of these powerful people. As he did so, he nearly knocked his dad's glasses off. A moment later he put a finger into his dad's mouth and was pulling his lip down. This wasn't some powerful and prominent executive or politician; this was "Daddy!"

Whenever Jesus refers to God our Father as Abba, the image of that little boy jumping onto his daddy's lap comes to mind. And this, I believe, is what Jesus had in mind when He spoke of God as "Abba" Father. We don't have to be afraid of Him; He is not distant and aloof, someone to be feared. He is "Daddy!" He loves us infinitely more than a parent can love a child! We don't have to be afraid to approach Him; we can come bursting into the room, jump in His lap, knock His glasses off (Oops! Sorry! God doesn't need glasses!), and rest in His loving arms.

What a comforting thought!

HIS MOTHER'S GIFT

I HAD JUST recently been reassigned to another parish and was feeling rather useless and lonely. When I would answer the phone, the caller would ask, "Is Father (the pastor) in?"

When I would say no, the caller would ask, "Is the secretary there?" If she were not there, the next question would be, "How about the housekeeper (In those days each rectory usually had one)?"

When I would reply, "I'm sorry, she's not here either. Can I be of assistance?" the usual reply would be, "No, thank you, Father, I'll call back later."

Such conversations didn't do much to instill self-confidence in me. If only I could have appreciated those carefree days when no one seemed to need me!

After a few weeks of being the new assistant who no one felt was competent to be of service, I was delighted one afternoon when a young couple dropped by and asked what they had to do to get married in our church. What a joy to have someone come to me for help!

I explained our premarriage program to them and reserved a date for their wedding the following June. During the course of the next ten months I met with them a number of times, sharing my great wisdom about marriage and helping them plan their wedding. During the course of these sessions we became friends. In fact, I was one of the first to be told, about eighteen months after witnessing their wedding, that they were expecting; they told me even before they informed his parents, which I felt was quite an honor.

I baptized their son just a few weeks before I was transferred to another parish some 160 miles away. The next couple of years passed quickly as I was busy teaching full-time in our parochial high school, conducting adult religious education programs, and was involved in all kinds of parish work. Being so busy and so far away from the previous parish, I gradually forgot about the folks I had left behind.

About a year and a half into my new assignment, I received a phone call one evening from the mother of this couple whose marriage I had witnessed. She asked me to pray for her daughter, who had just been diagnosed with ovarian cancer.

Although I no longer had an obligation to minister to her, I took the occasion to drive 160 miles to visit her in the hospital. During the course of the next eight months I made a number of such visits.

The prognosis was not very good; she was obviously dying and knew it. During one of my visits, she was very depressed and discouraged. She loved her husband and child so very much and couldn't bear the thought of leaving them. She told me that her greatest cause of grief was the realization that her two-year-old son would not remember her.

Perhaps it was a moment of grace or an inspiration from the Holy Spirit, but after hearing her make this statement and sitting quietly for a while, not knowing what to say, I finally asked, "Have you ever considered writing a letter to your son and telling him how much you love him?"

She made no response, but she did take the suggestion to heart. She spoke with her mother about it, and her mother went out and purchased a beautiful, leather-bound journal. From that day on, whenever she felt well enough to do so, she wrote to her son in her journal.

She wrote about her own childhood, how she met her husband, his dad, and how much she loved him. She wrote about their wedding day. She wrote about the joy she and her husband felt when they discovered that they were going to have a child. She told him how much she loved him and how proud and excited she was the first time he rolled over, took his first steps, and said his first words.

She told him how much she was going to miss him and his dad, and she expressed the hope that as he was growing up and during his teenage years he would always listen to and obey his dad. She told him she would be watching him from heaven and hoped that he would always live his life in such a way that she could be proud of him.

She told him that she would be waiting in heaven for the day when his dad, her husband, would complete his life's journey and she could welcome him into God's kingdom in heaven. Together they would be waiting for him to join them.

At the vigil service the night before her funeral, many passages were read from her journal. Although the church was filled to capacity, one could have heard a pin drop. Nor was there a dry eye in that church.

Life goes on. After attending her funeral, I returned to my parish and became absorbed in my work. Every so many years I was reassigned to another parish. Perhaps once a year something would trigger a memory of this woman and her journal, and I would wonder how her husband and son were doing, offering a brief prayer for them.

Some thirty years later I was attending some social gathering when a woman came and introduced herself to me. During the course of our conversation she asked me if I remembered the lady who had written the journal to her son. I assured her that I did. She then invited me to come with her. She wanted to introduce me to someone.

The person she wanted me to meet was the son for whom the journal had been written. As soon as she introduced me to him, a man of thirty-three or thirty-four years, the first thing he said was, "You are the priest who encouraged my mother to write her journal. Thank you for doing that!"

He then proceeded to tell me that he did not remember his mother. He wasn't quite three years old when she died, but he went on to say that his earliest childhood memory is that of sitting on his dad's lap while Dad was reading the journal to him. He went on to tell me that he practically memorized that journal and that it has had a profound influence upon his life.

"You know, Father," he said, "it may sound rather strange, but in some ways I think I knew my mother better during my teenage years than my high school classmates who still had their mothers. I've always been very much aware of her presence and feel that she truly is watching over me."

He then went on to tell me that his dad remarried some years after his mother died and that he had a half brother and half sister. He himself was married and had two beautiful children.

As I drove home that night from that gathering, I spoke with his mother in prayer and assured her of what she already knew: Her son did remember her, he was very much aware of her presence, and she was a guiding influence in his life.

FATHER JOSEPH A. MIKSCH

WHAT'S IN IT FOR ME?

IN MARK'S GOSPEL, Peter says the following to Jesus: "We have put aside everything to follow you!" to which Jesus said the following in reply:

> I give you my word, there is no one who has given up home, brothers or sisters, mother or father, children or property, for me and for the gospel who will not receive in this present age a hundred times as many homes, brothers and sisters, mothers, children and property—and persecutions besides—and in the age to come, everlasting life. (Mark 10:28-31)

I remember so vividly the night before I left home for the seminary. I stayed out in the field late that night, plowing under wheat stubble. Knowing that it would be the last time that I would be sitting on a tractor for a long time, I didn't want to quit. I was in a very melancholy mood, thinking to myself of all that I was giving up—family, home, and all of my friends. Leaving home for the first time is never easy! I remember thinking, "God, I'm giving up everything to follow You!" I didn't repeat Peter's statement: What's in it for me? But it certainly was there in the back of my mind.

It was difficult leaving home for the first time and leaving family and friends behind. It continues to be difficult for me whenever I have to pack my bags and move on to another assignment. I become very close and attached to the people whom I serve in a parish. As a priest, I am privileged to share in the high and low points in people's lives. Frequently, I'm among the first to hear their good news. A couple, whom I prepared for marriage and whose marriage I witnessed, often shares with me the good news that they are expecting; sometimes they call me even before they have notified family members. I'm often among the first to see the newborn in the hospital and have the joy of welcoming that child into the church through baptism.

In times of sickness and tragedy, I'm often the first to be called to the scene of the accident or to the hospital. Frequently I am there to greet other family members as they arrive. Often I form very close bonds with people who are preparing for death, as well as with their families.

As a result, I form very close relationships with my people and become very much a part of their family. Doors are opened to me, and I can drop in unannounced at almost any time and feel very much at home with people.

People often share very openly with a priest the crosses and difficulties they are carrying. Through the sacrament of reconciliation they share their sins. I've had individuals tell me after they had confessed their sins that what they had just shared they never thought they would be able to share with another human being. When people entrust to me the secrets of their lives, or their most personal sins, I am so deeply touched by the trust they have placed in me, and I feel so very privileged to be so trusted. I have never thought less of someone when they share so intimately with me, rather I find myself responding with gratitude and love for the trust they have placed in me.

I used to wonder why I felt this way when people shared what they considered to be their ugliness, their sinfulness; then one day I came to understand. We are all created in the image and likeness of God. When a person is totally honest and shares who he truly is, even though he may be sharing his badness, the image of God shines through.

When one is privileged to share so intimately in people's lives, it becomes extremely difficult when it comes time to say good-bye, to move on to another parish. One weekend you look out over the congregation and know everyone there; the next weekend you look out over a new congregation and know absolutely no one. As a result, such transitions can be times of intense loneliness. Having made such moves ten times in my life, I have come to realize that I go through a grieving process each time I move. Usually it takes about a year in a new assignment before I suddenly feel at home.

While such transitions are painfully difficult, they are also exciting. I think of each such assignment as the beginning of a new chapter in the story of my life. When first in a new assignment, I find myself asking people: Who is that? Within a couple of years, parishioners who have lived their entire lives in that parish will be asking me, pointing to another parishioner: Who is that?

As pastors in a parish, we have so many opportunities to meet people and enter into new relationships. Any time the doorbell or telephone rings it can be the beginning a new, lifelong friendship.

Thus, while a transfer from one parish to another can be a gut-wrenching experience, I've learned that one never leaves true friends behind and now one has an opportunity to make many new acquaintances.

FATHER JOSEPH A. MIKSCH

Sometimes I am also filled with wonderment after I move on to another parish. It's happened a number of times that people who gave me the most trouble, were critical of every decision I made, and never seemed to have a good thing to say are the ones who hang on when I moved to another parish, and continued to come to seek my advice or spiritual direction.

While adjusting to my new surroundings in one parish and dealing with many parishioners who had problems and difficulties, on one particular afternoon I was feeling physically and emotionally drained. I missed the security of my previous assignment, and I missed the people I had left behind. The phone rang. This time the caller wasn't calling to ask something of me, rather she began by introducing herself, and then saying, "Father Joe, how are you? My husband and I noticed that you looked awfully tired and worn out at Mass this morning. Are you okay? I'm just calling to let you know how happy we are to have you as our new pastor. If there is anything we can do for you, please let us know."

I can't tell you how much that phone call meant to me. After it was over, I cried tears of joy! So many people had been coming to take from me; it was so comforting to know that someone cared! The members of that family became, and still are, among my closest friends.

Although the first year in a new assignment is usually a long and difficult one because one has to learn so many new things and try to figure out how things work, usually after about a year I will find myself driving back to the rectory and suddenly realize that it is "home." After that, each year flies by more quickly.

What is exciting about beginning anew is that one has an opportunity to enter into so many new friendships. As priests we have so many opportunities in which to meet people. When one first arrives in a parish, you find yourself asking, "Who is that? What was his name?" One year later, people who have lived their entire life in a parish will be asking you, "Who is that? What was his name?"

I've learned a wonderful lesson from the woman who called me to ask how I was doing. That small gesture and expression of concern meant so much to me. I now try to emulate her example.

Teaching in the local high school, one of my students had a sister who was dying of cancer. I noticed that she was often inattentive in class, so one night I wrote a brief note to her and put it on her desk. I expressed my concern for her, stating that I knew how difficult it must be for her to concentrate when her sister is so ill. I told her that I was available if she ever needed to talk and assured her that I was praying for her sister and for all the members of her family.

I placed the card on her desk next day. She read it before class. After class, she waited until her classmates had left the room; then she walked past my desk and simply said, "Thank you, Father Joe, for the note."

Being a shy girl, she never did stop by to visit with me, but she obviously shared the card with her parents. As the end drew near, her parents asked me to come to visit their daughter even though I wasn't their pastor. On the afternoon that she died, I was the first one the family called, and when I arrived, I was asked if I would preach the homily at the funeral liturgy. We have been friends ever since.

Sometimes the smallest gestures or expressions of concern make all the difference in another's life. As priests we are privileged to have so many opportunities to make such gestures and thus become involved in the lives of so many people. Thus, painful as transitions from one parish to the next may be, such transitions provide one with so many opportunities to expand one's horizons and to make so many new and wonderful friendships.

Today, as I reflect back over my life as a priest, I often think back to that night when I was plowing under wheat stubble. I think to myself how dull and uninteresting my life would have been if I hadn't left home and gone to the seminary to become a priest. Being a quiet and shy person by nature, I probably would have gotten some simple job; perhaps I would have married and settled down to a rather quiet and uninteresting life. My circle of friends would have been very small and my life rather routine.

By leaving home, family, and friends behind, I truly have received many hundreds of families and friends. I feel very much a part of so many families, I can't begin to count the number of friends I have. I have so many opportunities and doors open to me that would never have been opened to me had I not become a priest. Most important, I have the satisfaction of knowing that I have an opportunity to touch the lives of people and truly make a difference!

FATHER JOSEPH A. MIKSCH

A CHANCE TO BITE AN ARCHBISHOP!

GROWING UP ON a farm, we always had a dog, lots of cats, and tame rabbits. I no longer recall how it was that I got my first tame white rabbit, but I certainly was delighted to have him for a pet. Seeing the poor bunny hopping around all alone, I finally persuaded my parents to get another "male" companion to be with him. Apparently we made a mistake in getting that second "male" rabbit. Soon we had rabbits galore!

Once they numbered over fifty, Dad issued orders that we needed to do something before they took over the farm. We sold rabbits, we ate them, and we gave them away until finally our farm was rabbit-free. Or so we thought! One pregnant mother had burrowed underground, as was their custom, and produced another litter. Soon rabbits were again taking over.

This time we just opened the pen and let them run free. For several years tame rabbits of various colors roamed about the farm buildings and nearby fields before they finally disappeared.

Our dogs came in all shapes and sizes, but my favorite was a German shepherd. That dog was definitely "my dog." We would wrestle together and roll around on the ground in vicious combat; he would growl ferociously and snap furiously at me, but never bit me. When a stranger drove onto the place, however, that was a different story! No one ever got out of the car until someone called off the dog.

Sometimes when the dog was sleeping in the frontyard, I would sneak out the back door dressed in a long coat and hat, walk out the long driveway, and make a lot of noise. The dog would wake up and come bounding out the driveway, ready to tear the intruder to pieces. When he was just a few feet away, I would throw off the hat and coat and call him by name. Instantly his furious growls would turn into apologetic whimpers as he would jump up and lick my face.

Although I loved animals as a boy growing up on the farm, I never cared to have pets in the house. To my way of thinking, people live in houses, and animals need freedom to roam around outside in broad, open spaces. Often as a priest I am invited to people's homes where a dog is considered to be a member of the family. Invariably, no matter where I choose to sit, the dog will come and want to befriend me, jumping up and crawling all over me. Although family members may think it's wonderful that the family dog has taken a liking to me, it's affection I could do without.

On the other hand, I guess it's better if a mutt takes a liking to me! I remember visiting one family whose big mangy hound obviously did not like me. While I sat on the sofa, he sat a few feet away, growling and showing his teeth. If I made the slightest move, he stood up, ready to pounce. I didn't find his master's words very comforting: "Don't worry, Father! He won't hurt you!" I didn't go back to visit these people a second time!

In smaller parishes a priest not only gets to know all of his parishioners by name, but also gets to know a lot of dogs by name. I'll never forget Kolby. An elderly widow in the parish had invited me over for dinner that evening so that I could meet her grandson who was visiting her. She had spent the entire afternoon preparing the meal and baked my favorite pie for dessert. Unfortunately, she didn't know what kind of thieving mutt Kolby, her grandson's old dog, was.

As she came to the front door to greet me, Kolby bounded into the kitchen, took a mighty leap up onto the counter, and gulped down the entire pie in a matter of seconds. So much for our dessert! I felt no sympathy for the beast when later I learned that he wasn't feeling well.

Then there was Pepsi, the only bilingual dog I ever met. He could understand his master's commands in both English and Polish.

By far the meanest dog I've ever known was Barney. A dog with character, Barney seemed to have developed a deep hatred for people early in life and would attack anyone without the slightest provocation.

Barney lived near the parish hall, which was about two blocks from the rectory. A huge sign, which bolstered Barney's nasty image, was displayed in front of his doghouse; it read: BEWARE OF DOG! Anyone who ignored that sign paid dearly for that mistake.

Barney wasn't just a mean old junkyard dog.

He had class! For example, when Barney would cut across the lawn in front of the rectory on his way to visit his owner's in-laws, he would never growl or show his

FATHER JOSEPH A. MIKSCH

teeth until he was safely on public property. No matter how much I would yell at him, Barney would trot quietly across the lawn until he came to the street. Then he would turn around, and snarl and growl fiercely.

While Barney lived near the parish hall, few people dared to walk up the lane in front of his house for fear of being attacked. Some folks even accused his owner of hiding in the woodshed and yelling "Sic-um!" as they approached.

One year when the archbishop came to administer the sacrament of confirmation, the parish planned to celebrate with a potluck dinner in the old hall after the Confirmation service. I offered to give the archbishop a ride to the hall for dinner, but he insisted on walking, being totally unaware of Barney's presence. As I accompanied him to the hall along with several other priests, I suddenly remembered Barney. If Barney were home, he too would celebrate by biting someone.

Not knowing what to do and not wanting to appear to be a coward, I finally concluded that poor Barney had never had an opportunity to bite an archbishop, so we continued on our journey, though I did stay to the left on the far side of the road from Barney's house. If Barney were home and did attack, I felt I could run more quickly for help from that side.

As it turned out, Barney was not home that evening, and the archbishop and priests made it safely to the hall, totally unaware of the potential danger they had just faced, and poor Barney missed the opportunity of a dog's lifetime, the chance to bite an archbishop.

Then there was Curlie, the neighbor's big tomcat. Curlie lived just across the street from the church. One entered the church through glass doors on the south side of the building. During the winter months Curlie would lie in front of the church, soaking in the warm rays of the sun. Every now and then a sparrow would fly into the glass doors, which reflected the surrounding area. Stunned by the impact, the birds would fall to the sidewalk, and before they could recover, Curlie would pounce upon them and enjoy a tasty meal.

LET GO BEFORE LIGHTNING STRIKES

I T HAD BEEN thirty-one years since I last hiked to the divide. Then a young man in my prime, the 7.7-mile hike with a five-thousand-foot altitude gain was just a stroll through the woods. I could cover the distance in less than two hours carrying a backpack, mattock, and cruiser ax. Now, thirty-one years later, I felt I was doing good to cover the distance in four and a half hours.

The lines from William Wordsworth's poem *Lines Composed a Few Miles above Tintern Abbey* became a mantra running through my mind as I hiked up the canyon trail:

> Five years have passed; five summers, with the
> length of five long winters! [Not five, but thirty-one!]
> And again I hear these waters,
> Rolling from their mountain springs
> With a soft inland murmur.
> Once again do I behold these steep and lofty cliffs,
> That on a wild secluded scene impress
> Thoughts of more deep seclusion,
> And connect the landscape with the quiet of the sky.

Instead of carrying a mattock and cruiser ax, I was carrying two aluminum ski poles. I discovered several years earlier that ski poles relieve much of the pressure on one's legs when hiking up steep trails, and take the strain off one's knees when descending.

The plan for the day was to hike to the divide, then scramble another half mile and five hundred feet up to the top of Static Peak. Although not considered to be a technical climb in any sense of the word, Static Peak does offer one a commanding view of some of the major peaks to the north in Teton Range. The view from the summit would provide a magnificent photo opportunity.

Huffing and puffing, I plodded on toward the divide with my companions. Thirty-one years of sitting behind a desk, teaching in a classroom, and visiting the sick, had certainly begun to take its toll. Still I was pleased with my physical condition.

As we approached the divide and looked up toward the summit of the peak, now seemingly very near, I began to worry about the dark clouds that drifted ominously overhead. While they didn't seem to pose an immediate threat, I knew that they could build rapidly, and lightning could become a major threat to anyone high on the exposed peak. I also knew that Static Peak wasn't given its name without a reason.

I had been caught once on the very summit of a Teton peak in an electrical storm and hope I will never have such an experience again. With every hair of my head being pulled upward, ice ax, pitons, and carabiners aglow with St. Elmo's fire, and the rocks buzzing from static electricity in the air, I felt my life was about to come to an end at any moment with the next bolt of lightning. Never before had I prayed the Hail Mary with such fervor—"pray for us sinners, *now* at the hour of my death!"

Thus, when we arrived at the divide, after a brief assessment of the cloud formations, I suggested that we forget about going on to the summit. It would have taken us at least an hour to reach the summit and return to the divide. At the rate the clouds were building, we could be in serious trouble so high on the mountain.

We did rest a bit, took pictures, and were ready to pose on some nearby rock formations for some "exposure shots" when suddenly a streak of lightning streaked from a nearby cloud and struck the valley floor nearly a mile below, followed by a deafening clap of thunder. A similar dark cloud drifted directly overhead less than a thousand feet above. It was time to descend, and we began immediately.

Crossing several steep snowfields, we scampered carelessly down shortcuts between switchbacks in the trail. As we retreated down the steep mountain slope, I suddenly realized that I was carrying two aluminum ski poles or "portable lightning rods"—not a bright thing to do under such conditions!

Common sense told me that I should immediately throw them as far away as possible! But gee, I had paid $2 for them at a garage sale, and I knew they would come in handy on the long hike down the steep trail. So I clung to them, rationalizing that I could throw them away as soon as I began to feel that tingling sensation in my hair caused by static electricity.

Fortunately, although there were further peals of thunder nearby, we descended the mountain safely and wearily hiked out to the parking lot.

It was only much later as I began to reflect back upon this experience that I began to realize how foolish I had been. Common sense told me to discard those ski poles immediately, but I clung to them greedily and in so doing endangered my life. How foolish!

The more I reflected upon my actions, the more I realized how often I have done the same with my spiritual life. So often I have made foolish choices in choosing sin, which could endanger my eternal salvation. "I can always go to confession at a later date." "I'm so busy now, I don't have time to pray, but when I am older and retired, then I can prepare for eternal life." "Sure I want to overcome this habit of sin, but not just yet."

Yes! I would definitely throw my ski poles away if my hair began to tingle, but what if lightning were to strike first! Sure, I would receive the sacrament of reconciliation and pray to God for forgiveness with all the fervor of my heart if I were on my deathbed, but what if I die suddenly from a heart attack or get killed instantly in an accident?

My hike up to Static Peak Divide has caused me to do a lot of thinking. Reflecting back on the experience has made me realize that I need to make some changes in the way I live my life *now*! It's not so much the ski poles that I need to discard, but rather some of my sinful and selfish ways. Then, if lightning strikes, I will be ready to meet the Lord.

FATHER JOSEPH A. MIKSCH

SAINTS AMONG US

S OME YEARS AGO as I was adjusting to my new surroundings after a transfer, I was visiting with another man who had just moved into our community. He too was adjusting to his new environment. During the course of our conversation he said to me, "You priests are so lucky! You get to work with the best of people!"

The more I reflect upon that statement, the more I realize how true it is. We priests truly do work with the best of people. In fact, we often work with saints who live among us.

They are ordinary people—people who would blush with embarrassment if we referred to them as saints. They would be the first to admit that they are sinners. Yet by the grace of God they one day will be saints in heaven.

Some parishioners to whom I was privileged to minister are undoubtedly saints in heaven. I first came to know Saint Tracy Schmitz as a little two-year-old who had cancer. During the course of the next two years I saw her often at Sunday Mass. Her parents would always sit in the front pew and hold little Tracy throughout the Mass. The chemo treatments she was taking caused her to lose all of her hair, and often she did look like a very sick little girl.

When she was only four, just a few weeks before she died, we noticed that when her parents came up to receive Holy Communion, little Tracy would say, "Jesus! Jesus!"

Since she recognized that Jesus was present, we decided to give little Tracy Holy Communion too. There were many tear-filled eyes in church when people saw Tracy receive a tiny particle of the Sacred Host, and there wasn't a dry eye in church on the day of her funeral, but we all knew without any doubt that little Tracy Schmitz is now a saint in heaven.

Over the years I have watched so many husbands and wives caring for a sick spouse, sometimes for years, becoming virtual prisoners in their own home as they looked after their spouse suffering from Alzheimer disease or from a stroke. Never do you hear them complain or utter a word in self-pity, but they are always ready to do whatever they can for their loved one.

Sometimes I hear such people apologize that they can't do more for the church! I can only reassure them that they are serving the church in looking after their afflicted spouse in such a beautiful way and setting such a beautiful example of unconditional love.

I think of a young mother with two children. Shortly after she conceived a third child, she discovered she had cancer and a very diseased heart. Her doctor advised her to have a hysterectomy, which would take the life of the unborn child; he was afraid the cancer would spread too much if she waited until she could deliver the child and feared that her heart wasn't strong enough to sustain her through a full-term pregnancy.

There was no way that she was going to take the life of that child. Placing her complete trust in God, she carried the child to full term and delivered a healthy baby.

In an age when so many abort their babies because a pregnancy would be inconvenient, such a courageous, saintly woman stands out as a true hero and disciple of Jesus.

I see holiness in couples who have a severely handicapped child and the loving way in which they take care of it. In the Gospel of John, Jesus says the following: "No one has greater love than this, to lay down one's life for one's friend" (John 15:13). I used to think of this passage in terms of someone heroically rushing in front of an oncoming train to push a child to safety and losing his life in the process, but not anymore. Today I think this passage applies to parents or spouses who lay down their lives each day to care for a handicapped child or sick spouse. They receive little recognition for their heroism, and sometimes no gratitude, and yet they sacrifice day after day, sometimes for years, without expecting anything in return.

When I think of saints, I think of one of my friends, a man who is ninety-two years old. From the time he was in his early teens he was afflicted with muscular dystrophy and severely handicapped. While his peers grew up, married, and raised their families, he was confined to his home, where his parents took care of him, than a brother and sister. For the last thirty years he has been in a nursing home. In all the years I have known him, I have never heard him utter one word of complaint. He always has a positive outlook on life and always is doing things for others.

What does a man who can't even care for himself do for others? He collects religious magazines and, with the help of a doctor friend, sends them to prisons so inmates will have some quality reading materials. He collects pencils and small school items and sends them to the missions. He leads the people in prayer in the nursing home, leading the rosary and sharing the scriptures with them.

When I visit with him, I know that I am with a holy man, with a living saint!

On November 1, the feast of all saints, I think of Mark. I first met Mark when he was a freshman in high school. A big kid, 6'2" tall, and built as solid as a rock, he was a football coach's dream. Mark had long, flowing blond hair, which reached to his shoulders. Fortunately for the rest of us, he had a very gentle and pleasing disposition. Because he lived way out in the country and his dad needed his help on the farm, Mark didn't go out for football. He preferred to play his guitar instead.

Mark came from a large family. They always attended Mass on Sunday as a family and sat on the front pew.

I remember that, one Sunday night during my CCD class, some of the students were messing around. I finally blew my stack and in a very threatening voice declared that everyone had better shape up! I took a deep breath and stood as tall as my 6'1" frame would allow, declaring that I was big enough to throw out anyone who didn't behave. Suddenly, out of the corner of my eye I saw "big Mark" sitting in the back of the room and I realized how foolish my threat must have sounded to him. "Mark," I said, "I wasn't talking to you. You can do whatever you want in my class! Okay! I'll leave you alone if you leave me alone!"

Mark just smiled, and the tension in the classroom dissipated. I never did have to worry about Mark; he was always quiet and attentive.

One Sunday afternoon the following summer Mark was walking along the bank of the Missouri River with two of his sisters. Suddenly the bank caved in and his two sisters were being swept away in the swift current. Without giving it a second thought, Mark jumped in after them and managed to help them to safety, but Mark didn't make it.

Again I think of the words of Jesus: "No one has greater love than this, to lay down one's life for one's friend" (John 15:13). These words certainly apply to Mark, and I like to think that he is a saint in heaven.

I think of some of my elderly parishioners who are confined to their homes because of ill health and old age. They can scarcely see or hear; they can hardly get around. When I visit them, they tell me, "Father, I can't do anything anymore, so I just pray all day!"

My list could go on and on. As I think about these people, I realized the truth of the statement: "You priests are so lucky! You get to work with the best of people!" Indeed we do! We live and work with future saints.

SCANDALS IN THE CHURCH

IN HIS FIRST letter to the Corinthians, St. Paul compares the church to our human bodies, which have many parts. Each part has a special function to serve the good of the whole body. Paul then goes on to say the following: "If one part suffers, all the parts suffer with it; if one part is honored, all the parts share its joy" (1 Cor. 12:26).

How true are Paul's words! The whole church has suffered because of the scandalous actions of some priests. For this reason it is difficult to be a priest today; in some circles we are all suspect s and judged guilty by association.

During the height of the media coverage of the scandal of sexual abuse of children by priests, I was going to the hospital one day to visit the sick. I met a man in the parking lot and greeted him with a friendly smile and a "good afternoon!"

With a scowl on his face he snapped back, "Don't you even speak to me!"

As I continued on to the hospital, I began to sing loud enough for him to hear: "May God bless you with His love, always fill you with His love, may He hold you in the palm of His hand." I meant those words too. His comment, however, made me realize that some people today do feel that all priests are pedophiles who prey on little children.

It grieves me deeply! I spend a lot of time with children in the classroom, in the school lunchroom, and on the playground. Because parishioners generally have such a high regard for their priests, they pass on to their children that sense of awe and respect. They teach their little children to have a deep respect for God and Jesus, and to be quiet in God's house, and little children often conclude that the priest is God or Jesus. Thus, when I walk across the parking lot, they all come running and yelling, "Hi, Father Joe!" They place such complete trust in me!

The thought of betraying that trust and doing anything intentionally to harm them is to me unthinkable! I can't imagine anyone being sexually attracted to or desiring sexual contact with such innocent children. One truly has to be an extremely sick person to be so attracted to little children!

One can only pray for such people and wonder if perhaps they themselves must have been victimized as children to be that way.

My heart cries for those who have been molested and abused as children by priests. I know I can't begin to understand the pain, the sense of betrayal, and the mental anguish they have endured.

I became an altar boy when I was in second grade, which was quite an accomplishment when one considers the fact that in those days one had to memorize a series of long Latin responses. Thanks to the dedication, help, and patience of my youngest sister, I memorized all these prayers.

We lived three and a half miles from church. I remember one Sunday during the summer months when servers were not available. I volunteered to serve at both the 8:00 and 10:00 a.m. Masses. My parents attended the 8:00 a.m. Mass and then went home. I stayed in town and planned to get a ride home with my brother after the 10:00 a.m. Mass. I found it to be a rather exciting adventure.

Between Masses I walked downtown and bought a cupcake and candy bar. Admittedly, I was never a dainty eater. In spite of the fact that I have a big mouth, I managed to get some chocolate frosting on my face.

I was feeling really good about myself—like quite a martyr for volunteering to serve both Masses. Arriving back at the sacristy, I put on my cassock and surplus and waited for Father, a visiting priest who was covering for the pastor who was away on vacation. When he arrived, he took one look at me, slapped me gently across the face, and told me to go wash my face.

I was crushed! I had volunteered to serve both Masses; I gave up a good breakfast at home (though I really preferred the cupcake and candy bar) and in return I was slapped by a priest! A priest! I thought all priests were supposed to be so kind and gentle like our pastors all had been!

I never forgot that incident! It was such a minor thing, and yet it made such a deep impression upon me!

Then I think of what some priests have done to little children! I can't begin to imagine how they must have felt and how it must continue to affect them today. I can't begin to imagine how betrayed they must have felt. They were taught to have such deep reverence and trust in priests! How could anyone ever recover from such a horrendous sin!

Sometimes I find myself moved to tears when I think of what brother priests have done to little children. I so desperately want to run up to victims of abuse and tell them how sorry I am for what has happened to them, but I know that I can't. We priests are not the ones who can do that because they may never be able to trust a priest again! And I can't blame them for that! I can't blame any such victims if they hate me, and all priests, and declare us all guilty by association! They have every right to be angry! How could they not be angry!

I can only pray for them, and I do, asking God to touch them with His gentle healing power and help them come to know the peace that only He can give.

My faith in Jesus, the sacramental life of the church, means so much to me! I find such meaning and purpose in life in my faith in Jesus. Knowing that many victims of abuse may never be able to experience this because of what priests have done to them also causes me much anguish and grief. I can only pray that they will come to experience the peace and love that only Jesus can give, be it in another denomination, or if not in a church then in the silence of their hearts.

Although the scandal of priests has been well publicized by the media, I'm very much aware of the fact that, awful as the priest scandal is, it's only the tip of the iceberg when it comes to sexual abuse. In every community in our country there are victims of such abuse. With the decline in morals throughout our country, more and more children and adults are brutalized and molested.

To paraphrase Pope Paul VI: When we lose respect for one segment of society, all segments of society suffer. Or as St. Paul says: "If one part suffers, all parts suffer with it."

The church is not the only segment that has suffered because of the priests' scandal, the whole of society has suffered. All priests have suffered because of the scandal; we often feel that we too are judged to be guilty by association. Because of this, it's a difficult time to be a priest!

But it's also a wonderful time to be a priest! So many people in our society are hurting; so many are carrying unbelievably heavy crosses and burdens in life. As priests, we are privileged to minister to people's deepest needs and can proclaim to them a message of hope. One day, because Jesus died on the cross and rose again, there will be only joy, peace, and love beyond our wildest dreams and imaginings. It's this message of Jesus that we priests have the privilege to proclaim!

FATHER JOSEPH A. MIKSCH

EPILOGUE

A S PRIESTS WE have the greatest and the most exciting job in the world! Sure, some of us are lucky enough to fly airplanes and climb mountains. Yes! It's exciting to make an approach to a landing when you know your nose gear has collapsed! It's exciting to cling to a rocky mountain wall when every hair on your head is standing straight up, your metal equipment is aglow with St. Elmo's fire, and the rocks are buzzing because of static electricity! But none of this compares with the joys and excitement I have experienced as a priest! Witnessing the transforming power and presence of God in the lives of people, and experiencing miracles of grace—*wow*! Now that's exciting! Working with the best of people and walking among future saints—what an incredible privilege!

Yes! Being a priest today is one *fantastic vocation*!

CPSIA information can be obtained
at www.ICGtesting.com
Printed in the USA
FFHW021304190619
53090964-58733FF